The Untold Story

Gusii Survival Techniques and Resistance to the British Colonial Rule

Second Edition

John S. Akama

Copyright © 2018, 2019 John S. Akama
All rights reserved.

This publication may not be reproduced, in whole or in part, by any means including photocopying or any information storage or retrieval system, without the specific and prior written permission of the publisher.

This book is sold subject to the condition that it shall not , by way of trade or otherwise, be re-sold, hired out , or otherwise circulated without the author's or publishers' prior consent in any form of binding or cover other than it is published and without a similar condition including this condition being imposed on the subsequent purchaser.

First Edition: January 2018
Second Edition: July 2019

Published by Kisii University Press. (www.kisiiuniversity.ac.ke)

Cover Concept Illustration: Fredrick Onkware
Cover Design: Linda Kiboma (Second Edition)
Layout Design: Bethsheba Nyabuto (Second Edition)
Production Consultant: Nsemia Inc. Publishers (Second Edition)

Note for Librarians:
A cataloguing record for this book is available from Library and archives, Kenya.

ISBN: 978-9966-109-57-6

DEDICATION

To the memory of the many unknown Gusii warriors who died while defending their community against the establishment of colonial rule.

ABOUT THE AUTHOR

John S. Akama is the Vice-Chancellor of Kisii University. He was the founding Principal of Kisii University College which he formally led to acquiring a Charter in 2013 to become a full-fledged university.

Prof. Akama did his undergraduate studies in Education at the University of Nairobi. He then proceeded to the United States of America where he undertook Masters and PhD studies at Ohio State University and Southern Illinois University, respectively. On returning to Kenya he joined Moi University as a lecturer and rose to the rank of Professor, teaching at both undergraduate and postgraduate levels.

Over the years, Prof. Akama has conducted research and published widely in diverse areas such culture, sociology, tourism and wildlife conservation. His keen interest and research in the evolution, culture and history of the Gusii is reflected in this book. He is the author of *The Gusii of Kenya: Social, Economic, Cultural, Political & Judicial Perspectives* (Nsemia Inc. 2017).

TABLE OF CONTENTS

DEDICATION - III
ABOUT THE AUTHOR - V
ACKNOWLEDGEMENTS - XI
FOREWORD - XIII

PART I

CHAPTER ONE

BACKGROUND - 3

CHAPTER TWO

INITIAL GUSII STRUGGLES FOR SURVIVAL - 11

CHAPTER THREE

ADAPTION OF NEW MILITARY SKILLS AND SURVIVAL STRATEGIES - 27

PART II - 47

CHAPTER FOUR

GUSII RESISTANCE TO COLONIAL INVASION - 49

CHAPTER FIVE

THE 1908 RESISTANCE - 67

CHAPTER SIX

PRELUDE TO COLONIAL RULE - 77

CHAPTER SEVEN

OTHER FORMS OF GUSII RESISTANCE - 85

CHAPTER EIGHT

CONCLUSION - 93

LIST OF FIGURES

Figure 1: Battle Sites.. 23

Figure 2: Physical Layout of an Indigenous Kisii Homestead 36

ACKNOWLEDGEMENTS

Indeed, it is an inspiration to undertake this kind of research and be able to share pertinent historical knowledge concerning an indigenous Kenyan community with fellow Kenyans and the world at large. In particular, I always become energized when I find people who share similar interests as far as the study of indigenous African communities, such as the Gusii, are concerned. At the same time, I cannot lose cognizance of the fact that there are other people who may dismiss this kind of enthusiasm as unnecessary nostalgia concerning by-gone events that, at best, should not be taken seriously and, at worst, should be forgotten. To the latter group, I will only put across the Kiswahili saying which says, *mwacha mila ni mtumwa* (i.e., one who abandons his/her culture/ heritage becomes a slave others).

In this regard, I am indebted to like-minded Africanists whose work helped me undertake this historical elucidation on Gusii survival techniques and resistance to colonial rule. Special recognition goes to Robert Maxon of West Virginia University whose seminal work on the Gusii, in particular and Kenya in general, has really inspired me and acted as impetus for me to undertake this kind of study.

Furthermore, this study follows an Afrocentric approach. It provides a unique historical perspective on the underlying intricate historical and socioeconomic factors that made an African community (i.e., the Gusii) stand its ground in resisting colonial incursion and conquest. And they did this against all odds, and with determination and vigour. Within these general corpus of scholars, I would like to appreciate

Matunda Nyanchama of Nsemia Inc. Publishers and Christopher Okemwa of Kisii University for their works on the Gusii community that uses Afrocentric approaches. The works and their words of encouragement served as a booster to me while conducting this study.

Over the years, I have learnt a lot from many people from all walks of life concerning various aspects of the Gusii community. As a consequence, writing a book of this nature has made me crystallize some of the folk history and mythology regarding the Gusii heroic acts of resistance to colonial rule. I thank all those that have shared the Gusii experiences that have informed, directly and indirectly, the realization of this work.

I owe a lot of gratitude to the staff at the Kisii University, Vice-Chancellor's Office, who in one way or the other played a role in the development and final rollout of this book. In this connection, special thanks go to Jemimah Nyamweya, Gordon Ouma, Fredrick Onkware, Teresa Ntabo, Emily Onyancha, Okinyi Omambia and the staff at the Kisii University Printing Press. In the overall, I thank all the staff of Kisii University whose collegial attitude has, over the years, made my work at the fledging institution bearable.

Last, but not least, I offer special regards to my loving wife Marion Kwamboka, who always stood by my side, even in difficult situations; I also commend my children Bruce Orang'o, Teresia Nyakoinani and Larry Akama for maintaining family harmony, notwithstanding any shortcomings on our part as parents.

FOREWORD

Indigenous African societies thrived by deploying various survival strategies and techniques. Those societies that did not adapt to changing situations perished. In the case of the Gusii of Kenya, when faced with calamities and challenges, they either migrated to other locations or changed their social structures.

The Gusii, like most African societies, were confronted with countless challenges. Unlike today, when modern Africa is cushioned in neoliberalism, the many societies in the preliterate times migrated from region to region, in search of food and green pastures for their livestock. Migration was a survival strategy and food was a survival need, without which they could perish.

In this book, the author describes how the Gusii moved from Kano plains to Manga Escarpment, to Kabianga, to Trans Mara and back to Manga. When the ancestors of the Gusii settled in Kisumu, they realized that the place was characterized by unreliable rainfall and was prone to regular drought. As a result they moved to Kano Plains. Similarly, when they later came to settle at the hostile environment of Kipkelion, people became sick, animals died and crops failed. This made the people to call the place *Kabianga* (meaning "the place where everything refused") and, consequently, moved on to present-day Transmara. This migration was an innate survival skill of the Gusii which, in the preliterate days, enabled people to thrive and remain safe.

One other challenge the Gusii faced was war from their neighbouring ethnic groups, such as the Maasai, Kalenjin (specifically the Kipsigis) and the Luo. Here, too, the Gusii devised new methods of survival. One way of survival was to coin nick names or secret names for these neighbours, thus *Omogere* (Luo), *Omonyamato* (Kipsigis) and *Omomanyi* (Maasai). The use of coined names could not let the "outsiders" into the Gusii lives, secrets and strategies. The author explains that the Gusii built homesteads, *emechie* (singular: *omochie)* with security in mind. In general *omochie* had overall physical layout and design that took into consideration the safety and protection of the vulnerable members of the family, especially the children, women and the elderly.

Additionally, the Gusii had a system in which young men were raised with the conscious aim of 'protecting their community from enemies'. When they were circumcised, the young men were told in *esimbore* (male circumcision song) that *"rwana Sigisi, rwana Maasai* (go and fight the Kipsigis and the Maasai) - two hostile neighbouring communities of the Gusii. Although endowed with a sexual connotation, this song subliminally implanted in the youth a duty of sacrifice that awaited them after the initiation - that of protecting the community against her enemies. To do so, they were motivated by sayings such as the proverb, *"omomura kare sobo ne'rirubi nyamong'ento"* (a young man at his home is a King Cobra).

This implied that he was expected to fiercely protect his community and fight severely in the event of intrusion. In clans which slacked in protective strategies, young men were ridiculed, thus *"ensinyo ekona gotebwa bobo ne'yetari n'abamura"* (a border that is bedeviled by persistent skirmishes, is one whose clan has no young men). Nothing was as humiliating as the words and meaning of this proverb. This provoked young men to offer their lives for the community. Circumcision rituals, such as *ogokonga (ogokoma)* (drawing a spell or a curse upon another initiate) were other survival skills imparted to young men in readiness for the protection duties that awaited them.

The coming and establishment of colonial rule in Gusii are discussed in this book. Facing the colonialist was a challenge that provoked special resistance and survival skills from the Gusii. The people rose up against *ebango y'esaiga* (hut tax) and *ebango y'abasacha* (poll tax paid by men only) imposed upon them by the colonial government; they resisted the destruction of *chinsoni* (Gusii code of conduct) and the adulteration of *enyamumbo (a Gusii traditional movement which resisted Christianity and other European ways of life by the colonist)*, vehemently opposed *okirimiti* (the colonial oppressive working conditions) and aspired to keep the function of their *ebisarate* (educational centres for information education for young men and military training camps). Many Gusii people died in this resistance against the encroachment of the white man. They, however, managed to register their determination, resilience and power of unity, which, in a way culminated in the spearing of the British District Commissioner, Sir Alexander Northcote, by Otenyo Nyamaterere, the lead warrior of the Gusii.

Apart from this book, Prof. John Akama has also written *The Gusii of Kenya: Social, Economic, Cultural, Political & Judicial Perspectives* (Nsemia Inc. 2017). The latter captures, among other concerns, the Gusii Socio-Cultural and Political Organizations, Rites of Passage, Customary Marriage, Indigenous Medicine, Agricultural and Judicial Systems. The books are, not only a great repository of Gusii history and social-cultural values, but also a relevant resources for further research. Without romanticizing this past that is much spoken of, it is wise to note that one who knows where one has come from will know where one is going. So the past should not be obliterated by the modern concept of technology and green development. There is a lot to be said of the indigenous African past and much to appreciate of the same. Hence, by capturing the history and values of the past, Akama's two books negotiate the present and future possibilities of the Gusii people. I recommend the two books for researchers and students of history, anthropology, literature, culture and the arts.

Christopher Okemwa
Lecturer, Kisii University

PART I

Gusii origins and initial development of survival strategies

CHAPTER ONE
Background

Introduction

The scramble for spheres of influence in Africa (i.e., establishment of colonies) reached a crescendo in the late 18th century with the signing of the Berlin Treaty among Western imperial powers, particularly Britain, Germany and France. In that treaty, signed in 1885 following the 1884-1885 Berlin Conference, the colonists set out to establish total control over their colonial territories in different parts of Africa. However, it is important to note that when the colonial governments started establishing their control over the newly-created colonies, most of these territories were already occupied by indigenous African communities. The Gusii are one such group. These native African communities had settled and/or lived in these areas for hundreds, and perhaps thousands, of years. Furthermore, these communities had evolved and/or developed homegrown social, economic and political institutions of governance that were sustainable and were best suited their specific local environments.

In this regard, it can be enunciated that the indigenous institutions were a long-term and systematic response to various issues and challenges that the people had encountered over the years. Thus, the indigenous institutions and their roles were appropriately adapted to existing socio-economic and natural conditions. The indigenous institutions had withstood the test of time and, in all likelihood, they had served the African communities adequately over the years.

Hence, when the Western imperial powers started making in-roads into different parts of Africa, the indigenous people were not passive recipients of Western colonialism. This is because these communities had developed their own diverse ways of enabling livelihoods that were threatened by the invading forces. As such, the communities did not welcome the foreigners with open arms. They resisted, either overtly or covertly, the establishment of colonial rule over their territories. They perceived these external intruders as aliens who were out to destroy their communities and eliminate their long-held beliefs and socio-cultural values and principles.

One such community which, overtly, took up arms and fiercely resisted the establishment of the British colonial rule over their territory is the Gusii of South Western Kenya. This community is presented in the book as a relatively smaller community which was (and still is) surrounded by somewhat larger, and (largely) aggressive and belligerent communities such as the Luo, the Maasai and the Kipsigis. It is worth noting that these groups, unlike the Gusii, are non-Bantu. Situated in this position the Gusii had, over the years, developed diverse survival strategies to safeguard and protect themselves against external aggression from these communities.

It was these same survival and/or defensive strategies that the Gusii used to defend themselves against the British soldiers when the latter arrived in Gusii land in 1907. As they invaded the Gusii territory, the British soldiers ransacked Gusii villages, killing people, burning houses, raping women and capturing livestock as a way of subduing the so-called "treacherous Gusii natives" and placing them under the British colonial rule.

In this broad context, it is important to note that, in their initial encounter with the Gusii warriors in present day Mosocho region near Kisii Town, the British soldiers suffered massive defeat in the hands of determined Gusii warriors. In this initial attempt to place the Gusii community under colonial rule, the British soldiers encountered stiff resistance from the Gusii warriors that lasted for several months. This resistance led the British to rethink their strategy as they could not advance as they had initially planned. After being repulsed by Gusii warriors at the Mosocho battle, the King's African Rifles (KAR) soldiers made a quick retreat and took refuge in their newly-established base at Getembe (present-day Kisii Town) with the warriors in hot pursuit.

In the fierce encounter, the Gusii warriors almost overran the British administrative base in Getembe. Consequently, the pioneer colonial administrators, who had been brought to Getembe, had to relocate back to Karungu Administrative Centre, the colonial headquarters for the Southern Kavirondo region -- current day Nyanza region. As will be discussed in the book, it took several months before the KAR forces subdued the Gusii. And this happened after the soldiers obtained reinforcements from other parts of Kenya, such as Karungu, Kericho and Nandi.

However, this major historical phenomenon in which a contingent of relatively poorly-armed African warriors were able to resist and defeat heavily-armed colonial soldiers who had superior gun power with other accompanying military assortments is not captured in any historical records or government documents. Instead the colonial government's official narrative of this event is advertently slanted to give the impression that this was a minor skirmish between the Gusii natives and a few KAR soldiers. Consequently, this form of narrative is made to portray the Gusii community fighters as a 'disorganized group of Gusii native warriors' who then could not confront and defeat the well-organized contingent of British soldiers. Unfortunately, this same narrative has been entrenched over the years and/or is presented by most Eurocentric historians and other social scientists in their studies concerning the Gusii people.

Accordingly, the main aim of this book is to provide an accurate contextual analysis and historical presentation concerning this important occurrence of Gusii historiography and culture. In order to construct this critical narrative, the author has majorly utilized information as passed down by informed Gusii elders. These elders are largely the custodians of Gusii history and heritage. The author has also used archival records and his personal understanding of Gusii history and culture. We note that the specific section on Gusii resistance is largely adapted from Robert Maxon's (1989) narration of the event. Prof. Maxon is a prominent scholar on Gusii historiography and ethnography.

Further, within this broad historical context, there is a widely held narrative about the Gusii warrior, Otenyo Nyamaterere, which needs to be corrected. Otenyo is the famed Gusii warrior who bravely speared Sir Alexander Northcote, the pioneer colonial District Commissioner (DC). This false narrative holds that Otenyo was a deranged person who was high on narcotics when he speared the DC. This account, advanced by the colonialists, is inaccurate and misleading. On the contrary, as will be shown in this book, Otenyo was the lead warrior who commanded a large contingent of Gusii warriors against the KAR soldiers at Mosocho. He did so with extreme determination and courage. It is perhaps the fearlessness of this warrior that led protagonists to make inaccurate conclusions about him.

Perhaps, more critically, the Gusii warriors were able to stand their ground (using mainly spears and shields) against the British soldiers who were by far better armed. In this initial encounter both sides suffered heavy casualties. However, the Gusii warriors managed to repulse the enemy and were able to recapture more than 2000 head of cattle that had been confiscated by the British soldiers from villages in Bonchari and Kitutu clans.

Book Structure

The book is divided into two sections: *Military Techniques and Survival Strategies*, and *Gusii Resistance, Establishment and Impact of Colonial Rule*. The first section consists of three Chapters: *Initial Gusii Settlements as a Distinct Ethnic Community*, *Adaption of New Military Skills* and *Survival Strategies*.

Chapter One provides an introduction and structure of the book.

Chapter Two enunciates the movement of the Gusii into the South and South-western region of Kenya and how the community was inadvertently isolated and/or completely cut off from the other closely-related Western Kenya Bantu subgroups. The chapter discusses how the Gusii found themselves surrounded by relatively larger and hostile non-Bantu groups. The chapter goes further to show that finding themselves literally 'between a rock and a hard place,' the Gusii people found themselves staring at the unfortunate possibility of being annihilated as a distinct social entity and cultural group.

Chapter Three provides an articulation of how the Gusii developed new military skills and survival strategies that enabled them to effectively confront their enemies. These strategies included but were not limited to, positioning of groups of Gusii youths in strategic locations, such as hilltops and sloppy landscapes, to serve as scouts and/or harbingers who kept vigil on the possibility of approaching raiders and provide advance warning to the community. Second, the people made *eburu*, deep trenches that were dug round enclosed homesteads accompanied with *orwaki*, the construction of a wall that was also built around the homesteads. Further the community established *ebisarate*, military encampments where all able-bodied Gusii young men were stationed ready to confront the enemy, as the situation arose.

Section Two of the book consists of four chapters under the headings; *Initial Contact with the British, Initial Gusii Resistance, Prelude to Colonial Rule*, and the *Conclusion*.

Chapter Four indicates that when the British started entering Gusii, in the early 20th Century, the people had experienced a prolonged duration of peace and tranquility. This was after their success in fending off any form of external aggression. In this regard, the Gusii were living in relative prosperity and self- contentment.

Chapter Five captures the essence of Gusii resistance against the establishment of colonial rule over their homeland. The climax of the resistance was the Mosocho battle of 1907 where the poorly armed Gusii warriors were able to defeat and repulse a contingent of heavily armed British soldiers who had been sent to 'teach' the so-called 'the treacherous Gusii natives' a lesson.

Chapter Six enunciates the fact that after prolonged and spirited resistance, the Gusii eventually saw the futility of perpetuating the resistance. With the British forces better armed with superior gun power and capable of inflicting huge fatalities to Gusii warriors, Gusii elders called for a truce if only to prevent further loss of lives and possible annihilation. The elders had seen and experienced British brutality such as the burning down of whole villages, and shooting to death of hundreds of people including harmless women and children. Fearing extermination of the Gusii, the elders called a truce and let the British to triumph in conquest and establish colonial rule over the Gusii.

CHAPTER TWO
Initial Gusii struggles for survival against all the odds

Origins of the Gusii: An Overview

As is the case of most other pre-literate societies in Africa and other parts of the world, not much is known about the early history of the Gusii, particularly as concerns their origins and early settlements. However, based on lingua-anthropological evidence (i.e., existing linguistic formations), anthropologists and other social scientists postulate that the larger African group (the Bantu) to which the Gusii belong, must have originated in the Niger-Cameroonian region in Western Africa more than 3000 years ago (Shoenbron, 1998). Specifically, this is based on the understanding that it is in this very region that there exists most ancient Proto-Bantu languages and dialects. Further, it is enunciated that it was from this region in the present Eastern Nigeria and Western Cameroon where the ancestors of the Bantu people gradually moved and/or dispersed to broader areas covering Central, Eastern and Southern Africa. This movement was a slow process that likely took hundreds, and perhaps thousands, of years.

It is not our intention to provide a detailed articulation of the origins and/or cradle-land of the Gusii people. In any case, it is not the main subject of this work. However, it is understood that, about 1000 years ago, the ancestors of the Gusii and their close relatives, the Kuria, Suba and Logoli, were living at a place called Goye, in the current Yimbo-Kadimo region. From the area, the ancestors of the Gusii, Kuria, Suba and Logoli gradually spread and eventually settled in scattered parts in Urima, Ulowa, Sare and the Got Ramogi in present day Siaya County. It is worth noting that, due to many years of social interaction and acculturation, some of the pioneer Bantu groups (or parts thereof) were eventually assimilated by the Luo and vice versa.

According to Luo folk history, their ancestors had their first encounter with ancestors of the Samia, Bunyala, Gusii and Logoli in the Yimbo-Kadimo area over 800 years ago (Ochieng, 1974). It should also be stated that, probably, it was in this particular region that the current Suba evolved into a distinct ethnic community from that of the Gusii and Logoli who remained together. The ancestors of the Suba were the first group of these Bantu people to disperse from Yimbo-Kadimo region, taking south-westerly direction. They eventually settled in their current homeland in Homa Bay County, adjacent to Lake Victoria. Also, based on the reconstruction of existing folk history, the ancestors of the Gusii and Logoli for many years had close cultural and social interaction with the pioneer Luo ancestors, such as the Joka-Jok and Joka-Owiny sub-groups. Interestingly, surviving Luo elders in the current Got Ramogi area refer to the Bantu groups that they found already settled along the Yimbo-Kadimo Hills as the *Kombekombe* people. According to Luo folk history, the settlements of the *Kombekombe* were expansive, from the Yimbo-Kadimo to Usenge regions in the South and to the slopes of the Samia Hills in the North. It is also interesting to note that the current Kanyibule clan in Yimbo area traces its ancestry to a subgroup of the *Kombekombe* people who were assimilated by the Luo (Ochieng', 1974).

However, apart from existing folk history, there is scant information on the forms of social and cultural interactions that existed between the ancestors of the Luo and those of the Bantu groups such as the Gusii and other Bantu groups that had settled in the region. Notwithstanding the lack of clear information on the early histories of the Gusii and the other related subgroups, the contention that various Bantu families were dislodged and eventually driven out of the Yimbo-Kadimo region by the arrival of the Joka-Jok group of the Luo should be treated with caution. Of course, situations of increasing human population pressure on available resources (as appears to have happened in the Yimbo-Kadimo region during this period) may have led to localized conflicts and skirmishes between the Luo and their Bantu neighbours. This was as a result of each community struggling to make a living from available resources such as land, livestock and agricultural produce. In fact these forms of resource use conflicts are documented in the existing folk history of the Yimbo and other Luo clans in Siaya. In this regard, it is appropriate to state that the long-term relationship that existed between the Luo and their Bantu neighbours was more of mutual and symbiotic co-existence than outright enmity and conflict.

Consequently, it can be postulated that by about the year 1400 AD, the region around Yimbo-Kadimo and the Got Ramogi was experiencing population pressure relative to available sustenance resources (Ochieng' 1974). In this regard, various Bantu and Luo families dispersed to adjacent lands in Sakwa, Asembo and Seme region in search of (especially) virgin lands for agricultural production and human settlement. We postulate that, in this process of gradual dispersal, the ancestors of the Gusii and Logoli moved from the Yimbo-Kadimo and, eventually, settled in areas adjacent to present day Kisumu. Based on folklore, we estimate this period to be in the early sixteenth century. However, we note that due to unavoidable circumstances (as captured in the next section), the duration of settlement of the Gusii and Logoli ancestors ain Kisumu was relatively brief.

Settlement of the Gusii in the Kano Plains as a Distinct Ethnic Community

According to existing ethnography records and folk-history, it can be postulated that the Gusii evolved into a distinct ethnic community around the middle of the sixteenth century. This happened when they separated with their close relatives, the Logoli, in the present day Kisumu region. As it is presently, the region around Kisumu was characterized by unreliable rainfall and hence droughts were frequent. The ancestors of the Gusii and Logoli, who had originally moved from Siaya, found the place to be ecologically unsuitable for crop production and animal husbandry, which was their mainstay in earning livelihoods. As a consequence, the people experienced prolonged periods of famine and starvation in subsequent years.

The consequences were grave, leading to the separation of the Gusii and their Logoli relatives. Specifically, the separation was occasioned by severe famine and starvation, leading to their dispersal from Kisumu. The dispersion was characterized by abrupt movement of small clusters of people, comprising of closely-knit family members in search of food and other basic sustenance resources such as grass and water for their livestock. In this regard, clusters of Logoli ancestors moved north and eventually settled in the present Maragoli Hills, and; other small clusters of families that eventually became the current Gusii people took a south-easterly direction and eventually settled in the Kano Plains in the later part of the 16th century. Gusii folklore has it that, since the people who were moving away from Kisumu were in search of basic sustenance resources, the initial Gusii families were led by distinctive family patriarchs who were experienced hunters capable of feeding their families. Such patriarchs were strong-willed men with capabilities such as hunting to supply sufficient game meat for immediate sustenance.

Within this broad ecological and social context, it is worth noting that, during this period (over 300 years ago) the Kano Plains were a 'Park-Like Country', made up of tall savannah grasslands and ever-green acacia trees. These plains also teamed with a diverse array of tropical savannah wildlife such as gazelle, hartebeest, buffalo, bushbuck and wildebeest. This is where the Gusii families settled. In this respect, the Kano Plains provided an ideal hunting ground for the Gusii hunters. In addition, fish was plentiful in the many rivers and streams that crisscrossed the Kano Plains. Thus, although their initial intention was probably not to make permanent settlements in this area, these initial Gusii families created permanent settlements in the area. Thus, this must have contributed to the final parting of way for the Gusii and their close relatives, the Logoli.

It should be noted that by the middle of the 18th century, Gusii settlements extended to parts of Nyakach in the West and stretched further East to the Kabondo area. The settlements also extended further North to the slopes of the current Kipsigis Hills. During this period, the population of the Gusii people was relatively small, probably not exceeding 30,000 inhabitants who were broadly scattered in the expansive Kano Plains.

The Gusii practised mixed farming, rearing livestock and growing subsistence crops such as millet, sorghum, pumpkins and sweet potatoes to sustain their livelihood. In this regard, it can be postulated further that throughout their stay in Kano, the Gusii had an abundant supply of various sustenance resources. In turn, this led to rapid growth of population.

The Maasai menace and movement to the Manga Hills

By the mid-18th century the population of the Gusii in the Kano Plains had increased substantially, what with the abundance of livelihood resources. The larger population, in turn, exerted pressure on available resources. As a consequence, the people started to gradually disperse to surrounding frontier virgin lands in the current Eastern and Southern Nyanza region. Under this ecological and socio-economic context, the Gusii clans started to send harbingers to scout on the possibility of establishing new frontier settlements in the highland region situated to the south east of the Kano Plains.

The Gusii, however, were initially dissuaded from moving to the high altitude and mountainous landscape. This was due to the fact that the area was thickly forested and had extremely cold climatic conditions compared to the park-like Kano Plains, which had expansive open savannah grassland vegetation and warm temperatures where the Gusii people had led a leisurely life for many years.

However, it can be argued that the urgency to disperse to the adjacent high altitude areas was accentuated when the Gusii, for the first time, came into direct contact with the aggressive Isiria Maasai raiders coming from the Kamagambo low lands to the south east. It should be emphasized that the arrival of the Maasai in the Kano Plains completely destabilized existing political, economic and socio-cultural harmony that existed between the Gusii and their Luo neighbours. Unlike the low-level inter-clan rivalry that existed amongst the various Gusii clans, and the occasional inter-ethnic skirmishes with their Luo neighbours, the aggressive Maasai raiders were a different ball game all together. The Maasai had entrenched cultural beliefs that all cattle were of the birthright of the Maasai. This was without regard wherever the cattle were and whichever community had their possession. Driven by this belief, the Maasai would launch ferocious nocturnal raids on Gusii and Luo villages in the Kano Plains to capture the prized livestock.

Initially, the Gusii found themselves vulnerable to the Maasai raids that were executed mainly during the wee hours of the night. This is something the Gusii were not used to, as far as warfare tactics were concerned. In most instances, these night-time raids usually caught the Gusii by surprise. The Maasai raiders could make swift attacks, surrounding whole Gusii villages, burning down houses and granaries, and killing anybody who dared to challenge them. In the widespread misery and confusion that ensued, the Maasai would drive away large herds of Gusii livestock. In the event the Gusii warriors made counter-attacks to repulse the enemy, their cumbersome long spears and shields could not match the long-range bows and arrows used by the Maasai.

Consequently, the Gusii sought protection by hiding in the rugged Manga escarpment and the adjacent cascading hills.

It can also be postulated that another important 'push-factor' that might have contributed to the urgency of their movement from the open grassland areas of Kano Plans, was that the Gusii were now being sandwiched by two dominant non-Bantu communities (i.e., the Luo and the Maasai).

In these circumstances, the Gusii faced imminent danger of socio-economic annihilation and cultural assimilation. On the one hand, the marauding Maasai raiders were relentlessly attacking and killing people, capturing livestock and destroying any visible property (i.e. burning down houses and granaries). On the other hand the Luo, who were numerically superior, were increasingly impacting on the Gusii culture and lifestyle. Thus, it can be put forth that there was an overall realization of the danger of potential extinction (i.e., either annihilation by the Maasai and/or cultural assimilation the Luo). Clearly, the need for self-preservation must have contributed to the urgency of Gusii movement from the Kano Plains.

In this regard, with the realization that the odds were really against them as a community, members of the various Gusii clans decided to migrate to the secluded high altitude areas of the Manga Hills. To assure survival due to the prevailing hostile circumstances, the Gusii people moved together in distinct family units that were made up of closely knit kinsmen. Typically, each of these units was led by a distinguished family patriarch who provided strong leadership and security as need arose. This was mainly for security reasons and to assure unity in the face of the enemy. It was typical for members of the same lineage to turn to one another for assistance at times of emergency, for example when under attack from the Maasai. This would test the capabilities of the patriarch. The first Gusii group to move out of the

Kano Plains consisted of members of the Abagirango clan who were under the leadership of their renowned warrior called Tabichi. At first the group settled in the current North Mugirango location in Nyamira County before moving and eventually settling at Isecha in the Manga Hills.

The Abagirango were followed by members of the Abasweta clan, led by Manyatta, who moved past North Mugirango and eventually settled in the central parts of the Manga Hills near Ikuruma. Later, some Sweta families, consisting mainly of the Abasiango and Abasigisa lineage, moved further south to Tabaka plateau in the current Kisii County. Unfortunately, while in Tabaka these families were 'discovered' by the Maasai who once again started raiding their villages. In response, the Sweta families made a hasty retreat, retraced their way back north, and eventually settled in Nyagoe forest, south of the Manga Hills.

Later on, people from other Gusii clans also moved from the Kano Plains and settled in high altitude areas adjacent to the Manga Hills. They included families from the Ababasi and Abanchari clans who were led by Ogichoncho and Oisukia, respectively. Members of the Ababasi clan moved and settled in the Nyagoe forest, near the present Kisii Town. On the other hand, members of the Abanchari settled in the Marani area to the north-west of the Manga Escarpment. Note that some of the Gusii people remained behind in the Kano Plains, and, over time, most of them were assimilated and became part of the Luo. However, most of the Gusii families that eventually adapted to Luo culture maintained their original Gusii clan names such as Abagisero, Abanchari and Abasweta.

In their new settlements, the various clans quickly adopted to the new environment. In particular, the rugged highlands had many areas that were covered with dense forest vegetation[1]. The steep hills and elongated valley bottoms, to a large extent, provided an ideal physical environment for the protection of the people from external aggression. Clearly, the nature of the landscape was one of the fundamental factors that made the Gusii disperse from the open savanna Kano Plains.

The highlands offered a unique landscape consisting of cascading steep hills, escarpments, valley bottoms that were covered with dense riparian vegetation, and several rivers and streams that crisscrossed the diverse land. This was very useful in food production and, as alluded previously, the terrain provided protection against attacking enemies.

Thus, militarily, it cannot be over-emphasized that the rugged landscape was quite ideal for security and protection from external aggression. In this regard, whenever the Gusii faced any form of aggression from belligerent neighbours, the people would easily vanish and/or take cover in the depth of the forested steep cascading hills that also had several natural caves and cliffs. The people also took cover in the valley bottoms that were densely covered with impenetrable riparian vegetation.

Gusii warriors used the terrain well in confronting attackers. For example, it should also be noted that after everyone else had taken cover - especially the elderly, women and children - the Gusii warriors could, strategically, position themselves along specific defensive locations, such as the Manga

---

[1] This indigenous vegetation is no longer in place as it has been cleared over the years to make room for human settlement and agricultural production.

escarpment and adjacent hills. Here they would defensively challenge and repulse the enemy. Faced with the unfamiliar rugged landscape, covered with dense forest vegetation, the enemy could easily lose orientation and suffer defeat in the hands of the hardened warriors. Note that the Gusii warriors had one cardinal principle, i.e., not to cause unnecessary external aggression but to protect their people and property when need arose such as when they were under attack.

Movement to Kabianga and the Kipsigis invasion

As stated previously, most of the Gusii clans who had moved from the Kano Plains settled in Manga escarpment and the adjacent areas of Isecha Hills and Nyagoe Forest. These settlement patterns (i.e. various Gusii clans staying in close proximity with one another) were likely necessitated by security considerations. As already indicated, it was the ferocious Maasai raids that drove the Gusii into occupying locations that were strategically situated that could facilitate easy defense. Thus, the Manga escarpment, and the adjacent high altitude and forested areas, were ideal. Furthermore, the steep cliffs, raised escarpments and flat-topped hills enabled Gusii warriors to scout approaching Maasai raiders from a distance. This gave the Gusii warriors adequate time to position themselves in strategic sites along the steep escarpment to confront and attack the enemies.

Over time, the closely linked and concentrated Gusii settlements started to experience increased population pressure relative to the available resources. As a consequence, several segments of Gusii started dispersing to adjacent virgin habitats in search of new places to settle. For instance, several Gusii families from Manga-Isecha-Nyagoe triangle moved eastwards and eventually settled in the Kipkelion area, along the present Bomet/Kericho border. Due to unforeseeable circumstances, Gusii settlement in the Kipkelion area did not last long. The Gusii found the place to be extremely cold and not suitable for human habitation and the growing of their staple food crop, *wimbi* (finger millet). There were persistent crop failures that led to severe famine and starvation. Second, the area appeared to be disease-prone, as many people were affected by weather elements and started to die from pneumonia and other related respiratory ailments. Their livestock did not do well either.

Probably what finally broke the camel's back was the arrival of Kipsigis raiders in the area. Since famine and other forms of pestilence had already weakened the Gusii, the raiders easily overran Gusii villages and captured most of the livestock, women and the youth. This chain of calamities led the Gusii to become exasperated and distraught to the extent of naming the place "*Kabianga*", which literally translates to 'the place where everything refused. It is noteworthy that this place has retained the Gusii name till today despite that it is currently inhabited by people who are predominantly Kalenjin (Kipsigis) speakers (See Figure, 1).

Figure 1: Battle Sites where the Gusii fought major wars

Source: Author, 2017

As a result of the chain of calamities faced in Kabianga, various Gusii families started to retreat from the area, even as some Gusii families opted to remain in the Litein-Sotik area. Those who remained were mainly from the Tabori, Gusero and Basi clans. They were eventually assimilated by the predominant Kipsigis. Those who left took a south westerly direction from Kabianga. They passed through present-day Sotik, Geleglele and Ikorongo locations before eventually settling in present Trans-Mara District, at a place called Nyangarora. The place is named after a famous Gusii military leader Ongarora who was killed by Maasai raiders in the vicinity.

Life in Trans-Mara did not turn out to be as good as they expected as peace eluded them. Soon after their settlement in the area, the Gusii once more started to experience vicious Maasai raids. In a constant spirit of make or break, Gusii warriors led by Ongarora made a last ditch effort to fend off the Maasai. But when their gifted military leader was felled in one of the battles, the Gusii once again packed their wares and beat a hasty retreat from Trans-Mara, retracing their way back to their original settlements in the Manga Hills. It was in this hasty retreat that some families from the Abasweta, Abanchari, Ababasi and Abagirango clans lost track of their main Gusii families. These stray families eventually moved and settled in parts of present day South Nyanza. Eventually, they became part of the Kuria people of South Nyanza and Northern Tanzania. As they retreated from Trans-Mara, the Gusii were led by Oisera who took over the military leadership from his father, Ongarora. They retraced their way back into their original settlements in the Manga-Nyagoe-Isecha Triangle. By the early nineteenth century, most of the Gusii families were once again clustered around the Manga escarpment to the East, the Nyagoe forest to the South, and the Isecha-Rangenyo area to the North.

Perhaps due to lessons learnt from Kabianga and Nyangarora, when the Gusii returned to their original settlements, they became very conscious of their vulnerability to attacks from their warlike neighbours. The need for survival required that they be prepared to deal with future attacks. And it did not take long before they once again started experiencing attacks from the Kipsigis and Maasai raiders. The attackers made daring invasions into Gusii villages almost at will. For instance, the Kipsigis started to make incursions into Gusii villages that were situated in the frontier areas of Isecha to the north of Manga Hills, while the Maasai cattle raiders started attacking outlying Gusii villages in Nyagoe forest. In many instances, the Gusii had to make spirited counter attacks to repulse the enemy who seemed hell-bent on overrunning the Gusii. It was in this socio-cultural milieu that the Gusii undertook various defensive mechanisms to protect themselves against the enemy.

CHAPTER THREE
Adaption of new military skills and survival strategies

The following section provides an elucidation of the various survival strategies and techniques that the Gusii people developed and/or adapted, over time. We postulate that these techniques enabled the Gusii to fend off external aggression and hence assure the community's survival.

In response to potential extinction

Over time, the Gusii realized that they could be exterminated by the enemy groups surrounding them unless they changed tactics. This realization led them to change tactics and develop strategies that could help them fend off the enemies and ensure the community's survival in the long-run. In the process, they developed both military and non-military techniques that would offer a response to external aggression. As will be shown later, these strategies enabled the Gusii to turn around the balance and assure their survival as a distinct ethnic community. Furthermore, these very strategies and survival techniques enabled the Gusii to be able to stand their ground and resist the establishment of British colonial rule in their homeland.

First, the Gusii developed a strategy whereby young men were always posted in strategic frontier posts that were situated on hilltops. Whenever signs of approaching raiders were detected, the scouts could blow war horns to alert people in the adjacent villages of the approaching enemy. In such instances, Gusii warriors would leave whatever they were doing, and swiftly arm and camouflage themselves in strategic locations ready to confront the approaching enemy.

Second, since in most instances the Maasai and Kipsigis raiders were mainly after Gusii livestock, various Gusii clans identified specific safe place in which to hide the animals. These were reclusive caves, escarpments and sheltered valley bottoms. The locations were surrounded by steep slopes that were hard to access. In these places the Gusii could temporarily hide their livestock from probable raiders, especially during the night when most people were asleep.

Third, in order to protect themselves against nocturnal Maasai raids, the Gusii started constructing defensive systems that involved the digging of deep trenches around enclosed homesteads (allowing only one main entrance to the village). These defensive systems were called *chiburu* (singular: *eburu*). In other instances, the Gusii constructed *chindwaki* (forts; singular: *orwaki*) around their homesteads. Eventually, the people realized that a combination of the two defensive systems (i.e., construction of the wall combined with the building of trenches around the villages) were effective in fending off the enemy.

Fourth, members of various Gusii clans established military encampments, *ebisarate (*singular: *egesarate*), on the outskirts of the adjoining villages where all able-bodied young men were required to stay. They young men's age ranged from about 16 to 20 years. Here they were taught defensive techniques and spent time focused on defending the community against external aggression. Furthermore, livestock kraals were constructed around the *ebisarate* where all Gusii livestock was supposed to be kept, especially during the night. In this regard, Gusii warriors kept constant vigil in strategic locations, and provided requisite security and crucial protection to their families' cattle and other forms of properties.

Fifth, while previously the Gusii depended on spears and shields for fighting, they soon adapted new tools of war. They incorporated bows and arrows in fighting the enemy. The use of bows and arrows was more effective than the use of spears and shields. The latter were cumbersome and unsuitable beyond hand-to-hand combat. The new weapons were more suitable especially during times of extensive and drawn-out confrontation with the enemy. Gusii warriors now could fight using bows and arrows, which were easy to manoeuvre and could be carried for long distances.

These defensive initiatives appear to have been effective against Maasai and Kipsigis raids. Consequently, with the increase in human population in the original settlement areas of Manga- Isecha-Nyagoe, the Gusii people started feeling safe enough to spread and establish new settlements in other regions of the Gusii highlands region.

Finally, various Gusii sub-clans realized the importance of being united in temporary co-operative efforts, *amasaga* (singular: *risaga*), in order to undertake collective farming activities and effectively confront any massive external raids by the enemy. This required unity of purpose for the sake of collective survival. Specifically, in the prevailing circumstances, there was an urgent need for unity in order to be able to effectively confront external aggression and protect their resources from plunder. Particularly, following the lessons after being nearly vanquished by the Kipsigis at Kabianga and the Maasai at Nyangarora, many smaller Gusii subgroups decided to join the larger Abasweta clan for defensive purposes. It is in this context that the smaller Gusii subgroups turned to the Abasweta clan for military leadership (Akama, 2017).

Preparing the Gusii youth to be ready to defend the community

As indicated earlier, as they settled in their current homeland, the Gusii continued to face attacks from the Maasai and Kipsigis. The potential of annihilation as a distinct ethnic group became more and more real. The Gusii needed to change tactics if only to assure their survival. A critical societal issue arising was that of the security of the people, their land and livestock. Their strategy was one that could go beyond taking advantage of the terrain they had occupied and the use of *ebisarate* (encampments) for security of livestock and tutelage of young men. They needed to train the young men (warriors) who could defend the people. As such, from a very early age the Gusii youth, especially the males, were raised and inculcated with the cardinal principle of bravely and readiness to protect their families, clans and of course the whole Gusii community against any form of internal and external aggression.

In this regard, boys could start practising war skills very early in their lives. They were usually encouraged to perform mock fights with other boys from their neighbourhoods. In these mock fights, the boys learnt and/or acquired fighting and defensive skills, which they could employ in combat with the enemy. These skills eventually became handy in their later stages of life when the young men were called upon to put their lives on the line to defend their families, clans and indeed the Gusii community against aggression.

However, while undertaking mock fights, it was of utmost importance that the boys acquired other attributes such as group cooperation and teamwork when confronted with external aggression. One of the Gusii proverb states that *'nguba emo tiyana koira ng'ombe roche* (one shield is not good enough when taking cows to the river). Another one says *rosuka romo nduana kobuga* (one string will never make music). It meant that you needed cooperation of many people, duly armed, to effectively safeguard their livestock. These Gusii sayings emphasize the importance of teamwork, particularly at the time when people are confronted with difficult situations that require group effort.

The inculcation of these cardinal principles to the Gusii male youths became an integral element of rites of passage, specifically circumcision. During seclusion, which was a period of education and immersion in culture, the need for protecting the tribe was emphasized. Indeed, the military attribute of cooperation in fighting the enemy was central to this education. The circumcision rites were supposed to transition the initiates from the period of childhood to the stage of adulthood. Once initiated, young men were expected to take up their full mandate in society. For instance, as part of this, young men were expected to perform the noble duty of responding when called upon to protect the community and/or fend off the enemy whenever and wherever the community was under attack. Specific emphasis targeted at the belligerent Maasai and Kipsigis warriors, who were particularly after the priced Gusii livestock. It is worth noting that during initiation and specifically during seclusion period, the youths underwent various rigorous training and stringent rites that instilled requisite courage and stamina. These attributes would serve them well whenever faced with extraordinary and challenging situations such as combating cattle rustlers and other enemies. In particular, the initiates were inculcated with relevant skills as relates to confronting the enemy, tactfully, and being ready to pay the ultimate price, being ready to put one's life on the line defending the community as need arose.

As such, the practice of inculcating dutiful expectations in the youth was ingrained in the initiation process. Indeed, one can argue that the initiation of young men was, in part, military training to enable the youth defend the interest of the community. This is aptly captured in the magico-religious song, *esimbore*. This song *esimbore,* which was sung by youthful men while escorting the initiates to their respective homes, after facing the circumciser's knife. In it there was a direct call to the initiates to be brave and defend the community against aggression at all costs. The import of this is that, as young adults, they were expected always to be ready to face the enemy and defend their people. As a matter of fact, the magico-religious song amounted to a communal war-cry against the perceived enemies. It went as follows:

Ekegusii	**English Translation**
Oyo-oyo-o-o-o! Oyoo! x2	Here he is! Here he is! X2
Otureirwe itimo x2	He has been given a spear x2
Na nguba mbibo x2	And a big shield x2
Arwane Sigisi x2	Fight the Kipsigis x2
Arwane Bomanyi x2	Fight the Maasai x2
Arwane Sugusu x2	Fight in the North x2
Arwane Irianyi x2	Fight in the South x2
Arwane Bobisa x2	Fight the enemy x2

The Gusii also used the seclusion period to inculcate bravery in and strengthen the initiates' character, especially when faced with danger. Part of the training was the use of various techniques to test the initiates' level of endurance and courage. The process included applying acceptable methods of inflicting elements of pain to the initiates. For example, initiates could be stripped naked and their bodies could be covered with stinging leaves of certain herbal plants such as *enyanduri* and *rise* (stinging nettle). Other such tactics included submerging initiates' bodies in extremely cold water in the adjacent rivers during the wee hours of the night. Subjecting the initiates to these forms of pain and severe conditions of endurance were intended to train and make the initiates develop high level courage, tolerance for pain and stamina. These were seen as important modes of training that were aimed at moulding the young men to be able to withstand difficult situations and hostile environments such as confronting the enemy during times of war and/or being able to withstand various life threatening situations whenever they could occur.

In addition, during this critical period of seclusion the initiates received training of various war strategies and manoeuvres that they could employ when called upon. Examples, include battleground techniques, how to position oneself in the battlefield, how to respond to instant attacks by marauding cattle rustlers, and how to use and/or manipulate various types of weapons while in combat. Consequently, it was within this broad context of training to defend and fend for the community that the young adults learnt about the importance of discipline. They learnt that they were supposed to be highly disciplined and responsible adults, who were protectors of the community. In this respect, they had to ensure as much immediate protection of fellow warriors as well as for the community. As such, they were called upon to be ready to face the ultimate sacrifice, paying the ultimate price with their lives. They needed to understand that they could be killed while defending the community against the enemy. In this regard, by the time the initiates had gone through all the requisite initiation rites and rituals of passage, they were physically and mentally prepared to provide protection to their people, especially against external aggression and/or attack.

Perhaps more critical, young men who had successfully gone through these rites were expected to start living in the military encampments, *ebisarate* (singular: *egesarate*), in their respective villages. At these encampments they further underwent more specialized military training. A typical *egesarate* was made up of a number of huts, in which the men and boys lived. Here, they received specialized training that was provided by experts (usually older men) on various war skills and fighting techniques. The training reinforced the need for sacrifice and defence of the community, even at the expense of one's life.

Specifically as indicted previously, through strict supervision by experts, the young adults received further (more advanced) instructions and drills on how to handle and use various weapons, such as shields, spears, bows and arrows. Fighting skills were imparted on the young men by allowing them to take part in pseudo-fights with other young men from neighbouring *ebisarate*. However, the trainers made sure that each trainee was always alert, and that they did not cause injury to one another. Trainees had to understand that this was practice rather than actual combat.

Training at *ebisarate* went farther. Young men leant various skills such as how to make shields, spears, bows and arrows. Once the trainees were deemed to have acquired all the necessary military skills and knowledge, they were allowed to join other warriors during times of war.

At *egesarate,* the young warriors also had a duty of looking after cattle, both in the fields and cowsheds. In doing so, they were required to be always on the alert in case they were attacked. They were expected to detect the arrival of nocturnal cattle raiders. In general, it was only after they had served in various military regiments and graduated from the *ebisarate* that the young men were allowed to return to their respective homesteads and were now free to marry.

Gusii indigenous homestead as a defensive structure

The overall physical layout and/or design of the traditional Gusii homestead, *omochie,* took into consideration safety and critical security concerns. In this regard, the design of the Gusii homestead took into particular consideration the safety and protection of the more vulnerable members of the family, women, children and the elderly. It also took into consideration the protection of family property, especially the much priced livestock (See Figure, 2).

Figure 2: Physical Layout of an Indigenous Kisii Homestead

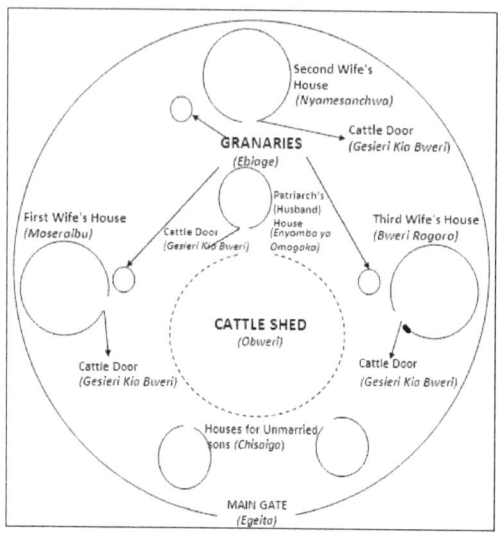

Source: Akama, 2017

In particular, livestock was to be protected from raiders who had a tendency of invading Gusii homes and/or villages in the wee hours of the night when the people were deep asleep. To put it emphatically, given any opportunity, the stoic cattle raiders could stealthily gain entry into the cattle-sheds and would quickly drive away livestock herds to their homelands.

It is worth underscoring how the Gusii homestead (*omochie*) was organized. It was headed by *omogaka bw'omochie* (the patriarch) who was typically polygamous. In this respect, the man's authority was law in the homestead and had to be adhered to by all, his wives and all unmarried children. It was typical for married sons to 'head out' and start their own homesteads (Akama, 2017).

The design and construction of the homestead was done with defence of the people (especially the weak; women and children) and livestock in mind.

In the overall, the physical layout of traditional Gusii homestead was circular in nature and had the following security features:

- First, the homestead had one main gate or entrance which in most instances faced the easterly or southeasterly direction. The placement of the entrance in that position was done deliberately with the realization that this was the most likely entry point by the marauding Maasai and Kipsigis raiders since their homelands were situated in that direction. Consequently, it was more likely to catch an early glimpse of the enemy coming from yonder. It was a defensive design that mitigated against people in the homestead being caught unawares. The direction of the gate meant that attackers could easily be detected as they approached the main gate. In such a scenario, immediately the enemy was detected, an alarm could be raised and the Gusii warriors would quickly arm themselves and run towards the direction where the alarm was coming from, while others would quickly arm and position themselves in the likely route to be used by the rustlers. Consequently, the Gusii warriors could wage a fierce counter-offensive attack to repulse the enemy and prevent them from taking away their livestock.

- Second, the houses of the unmarried sons were situated immediately after the main gate. The sons' houses were deliberately and/or strategically positioned for defensive purposes. In this regard, as per the layout of the homestead, the sons provided the first line of defence against intruders. Young men had a cardinal duty to provide requisite protection to the community, especially the more vulnerable members such as women, children and the elderly. Being close to the gate, the young people could be the first on their way out to prevent the enemy from intrusion and, in case of intrusion, they could rapidly respond accordingly as they were closest to the gate.

- Third, the cattle-shed was strategically built next to the houses of the unmarried sons and/or close to the centre of the homestead. This way, the young men could respond quickly were the enemy to reach the cattle shed. As well, placing the shed at the centre of the homestead made it difficult for the enemy to penetrate several layers in order to reach the livestock. As well, all houses of the patriarch's wives were built in such manner that they formed a protective wall around the homestead. In this regard, the overall physical layout of a Gusii homestead made it almost impossible for an intruder to gain entry, let alone reaching the cattle shed at the centre.

- Fourth, the main doors of all the houses in the homestead were built to directly face the cattle-shed in the centre of the homestead. Thus, the main door of the house was literally referred to as 'the door to the cattle shed' (*egesieri kia bweri*). It can be stated that positioning the main doors of all the houses to face the cattle-shed allowed members of the family to keep watch of the family livestock. Thus in principle, all members of the homestead were supposed to keep vigil and could raise the alarm whenever suspicious elements were spotted entering and/or getting inside the homestead.

Raising an alarm whenever there was a breach, particularly by women, could immediately draw the attention of young men (usually unmarried sons) in the homestead and those of the adjacent homes.

They could all quickly arm themselves with weaponry to confront the enemy. Given their training during circumcision and seclusion, and later in military encampments (*ebisarate*), the young men's response came without hesitation; and they executed the defence with military precision as they had been trained and as they had practised. In this manner, the people managed to protect themselves and safeguard their hard-won property from their enemies.

The Osaosao battle as turning point of Gusii Community

The outbreak of Osaosao Battle (also known by Kipsigis elders as the War of Mogor) was perhaps a defining movement for the Gusii and their survival as a distinct ethnic community. The account of this war features prominently in both the Gusii and Kipsigis folk history. It both communities, it is considered to have created a turning point in the Gusii-Kpisigis relationship, even as it entrenched the connection between the two groups. The war also marked a turning point in the Gusii defensive strategies. For the first time since their near-annihilation at Nyangarora, the Gusii were united, bound by a common oath and bound to their ancestral spirits and God, *Engoro*.

In the mid-1890s there was a severe outbreak of cattle pestilence (rinderpest) in the Kipsigis country. By 1895, the Kipsigis had lost almost all their animals to the pandemic. Thus, with the aim of replenishing their stocks, Kipsigis warriors started making regular incursions into Gusii. The area most hit by these raids was the Manga-Isecha-Nyagoe region. These daring invasions, initially, caught the Gusii unaware. With increased determination and confidence, as they made more raids, Kipsigis warriors started raiding villages beyond the frontier territory of North Mugirango. By

1896 the raiders were penetrating into the heart of Gusii country, spreading into the West and South Mugirango, Kitutu, Bonchari and Bomachoge. They attacked whole villages, burning houses and granaries and massacring Gusii warriors before driving away Gusii herds.

As was customary when the Gusii were confronted with an external aggressor, clan elders (*abakumi* or *abanguru*)[1] would convene to share thoughts and develop a response strategy. During the time of these raids, Nyakundi was the senior-most *omokumi* of Kitutu. He sent emissaries to summon other leading Gusii clan elders to a meeting at Isecha in Central Kitutu. Knowing the urgency of the meeting, all the *abakumi* converged in Kitutu to discuss the enormity of the danger that the Gusii faced. After serious consultation, the *abakumi* reached a consensus that the Gusii risked possible annihilation as a result of the regular Kipsigis attacks. As such, they needed a collective community response to assure the survival of the Gusii.

Following the discussions, Nyakundi led the gathering of *abakumi* in making a solemn agreement to unite all the clans and wage total war against the aggressors. He made the standard proclamation, *mwanchire twesi tochake esegi na ababisa baito Abasigisi* (have you all agreed that we declare an all-out war against Kipsigis)? All the *abakumi* responded in the affirmative by uttering the standard proclamation *eee twanchire!* (yes, we have all agreed!).

And they needed to do more beyond proclamation. All of them needed to take an oath that would bind them to the proclamation. Nyakundi, assisted by a famous Gusii prophet-leader, Sakagwa, led the

---

1   Sing: *omokumi* and *omonguru*

elders to the holy site, Ngoro ya Mwaga (Hole/Place of the Spirits) in the Manga hills. *Ngoro ya Mwaga* was a place where the Gusii performed sacrifices of all kinds. It was believed to be habited by ancestral spirits that mediated between the people and the God of the Gusii, *Engoro*.

Accordingly, the Nyakundi and the elders, and led in the spiritual process by Sakagwa, performed the necessary rituals that were meant to appease *chisokoro,* the ancestral spirits. In the process, they a joint declaration and took a collective oath committing their people to go to war with the Kipsigis. Thereafter, Sakagwa gave sacrifices to the ancestors and blessed the Gusii warriors who were soon to confront the formidable enemy.

Following this ceremony, the *abakumi* returned to their respective clans. Then they urgently summoned their respective clan councils, *chitureti* (singular: *etureti*). Their objective was to relay the message of the impending war against the Kipsigis aggressors. Afterwards, the war horns were blown all over Gusii country to inform warriors to arm themselves in readiness for an epic battle against the common enemy.

In 1896 Kipsigis cattle raiders were seen in the vicinity of the Manga hills in Central Kitutu (coincidentally, this place was adjacent to *Ngoro ya Mwaga*). Both Gusii and Kipsigis elders concur that a pitched battle took place that ranged along the Manga Escarpment and adjacent lands. In the battle, Kipsigis warriors were totally vanquished by a joint Gusii force. The pitched battles were so intense that the water of the adjacent Mogori and Charachani rivers turned red, saturated by blood from dead bodies of the butchered Kipsigis warriors that were dumped in them. Further, according to both Gusii and Kipsigis folk-history, a whole generation of Kipsigis warriors was wiped out.

The Gusii warriors were not done yet! They followed the retreating Kipsigis and slaughtered them to a man. They later took the war to Kipsigis territory in the Sotik-Belgut-Kabianga area. The Kipsigis elders concur that during this war their community lost most of their young men, a generation to be more accurate. Due to the unprecedented catastrophe, a younger generation of Kipsigis boys was hurriedly initiated into adulthood to inherit the many widows whose husbands had been massacred during the Mogori war and also marry the many young women that had come of age. In Gusii folk-history this was one of those defining happenings, perhaps the defining moment. In changing their tactics through unity of action, the Gusii (possibly) insured their survival.

The Osaosao battle is so engrained in the minds of Gusii elders that they still remember some of the victory songs the warriors sang on their way home after their victor over the enemy. One of them went as follows:

Ee sanyera abanto x3	(Unite all the Gusii warriors)
Ee sanyera x3	(Yes, unite)
Tokaga Mogori nero Ngarora[1]	(Don't think Mogori battle is the same as Ngarora)
Ee sanyera	(Yes, unite)
Ee sanyera abanto x3	(Unite all the Gusii warriors)
Ee sanyera x3	(Yes, unite)

Source: Personal Communication

---

2   Ngarora refers to an epic battle which the Gusii fought with the Maasai in Transmara, in which they lost to the Maasai after their leader, Ongarora was felled.

John S. Akama

The Gusii social model, chinsoni, for protection & identification

As presented elsewhere, by the late sixteenth century, the Gusii had evolved into a distinct ethnic community with unique social perspectives, political attributes and cultural orientation. By this time the Gusii had separated and/or had no direct links with their close relatives and Bantu subgroups such as the Logoli, Kuria and the Suba. In this regard, the Gusii dispersal from the Kisumu region and eventual settlement in the Kano Plains to the Southeast meant that the Gusii were cut off from the other Bantu subgroups. Consequently, Gusii people were sandwiched by non- Bantu groups, including the Kipsigis in the East and the North, the Luo in the West and the Maasai in the South. This was a peculiar situation that required cultural resilience, and social tenacity for the community to survive in the long run. Without such cultural resilience the Gusii would risk assimilation by groups such as the Luo that were more populous.

In this regard, the settlement of the Gusii at the Kano Plains was a turning-point in the history of the people as the Gusii, as an ethnic community, started charting their own destiny as a distinct ethnic community. Sandwiched among relatively larger non-Bantu communities some of whom were extremely hostile, the Gusii found themselves in a precarious situation. The people had to live with suspicion, mistrust, and skepticism with intense awareness of the neighbours' worrisome nature and tendencies. We realize that, indeed, in the duration of over 400 years, the Gusii struggled against all the odds to fend off constant attacks and undue social and cultural intrusion by these aggressive non-Bantu communities (Akama, 2017).

With the inherent realization of being surrounded by these large non-Bantu worrisome communities, the Gusii developed diverse survival techniques that they could utilize to overcome various natural and man-made calamities. As enunciated in previous section, some of these techniques were of military nature. Others were socio-economic and cultural in nature.

A major cultural strategy which played a critical role in keeping the Gusii community as a distinct and coherent community was *chinsoni* (Akama, J. S. 2017), the social principle around which all aspects of Gusii life dovetailed. *Chinsoni*, was a code of conduct that defined the Gusii community as a distinct ethnic entity. Adherence to *chisoni* acted to specify the Gusii as a unique social and cultural group. This social principle stipulated various ways in which Gusii people interacted and related to one another. *Chinsoni* regulated such matters of interaction across different generations, genders, social status and relationships. *Chinsoni* dictated people's conduct in any social setting starting from the homestead, sub-clan, clan and the whole Gusii community.

The concept of *chinsoni* was made up of sets of rules, roles and functions that guided the people's daily lives. This social model provided the people with motivation to undertake acceptable avoidance practices and behavioural restraint that were crucial in maintaining appropriate moral and social order. In that regard, the *chinsoni* code of conduct provided the people with an ideal social model that distinguished them from other communities. It guided overall Gusii behaviour and gave direction, meaning and purpose to the people's lives starting from the family or homestead level, sub-clan, clan level to the whole of the Gusii community. In the Gusii socio-cultural milieu, it was common practice that when people met in any social setting, the first thing they did was to inquire about the generation to which each person belonged and if there existed any form of family relationships. In this social context, people got to know their relationship with one another and the generation to which they belonged. This knowledge was fundamental in guiding their behaviours, approaches, interactions and treatment of one another. They thus knew how they should relate to one another depending on appropriate behavioural norms of restraints and familiarity as dictated by *chinsoni*.

Thus, an ideal Gusii social model was one in which people took pride in their unique social identity and moral conduct which promoted restraint and modesty as were contained in the *chinsoni* concept. Distinct from other adjacent ethnic community, the Gusii social model had a lot of prohibitions concerning accepted social behaviour and the manner in which people interacted and related to one another all the way from the family level to the broader Gusii community as a distinct social, cultural and political entity.

PART II

Gusii resistance, establishment and impacts of colonial rule

CHAPTER FOUR

Gusii resistance to colonial invasion

Introduction

The initial establishment of British colonial rule in the Uganda Protectorate in 1894 had little immediate impact on the Gusii and their lifestyle in the Gusii highlands region. In this regard, the Gusii were one of the last groups in Western Kenya to come under British rule. It was in the years 1900-1908 that the first direct contacts between the British and the Gusii, and the eventual colonial occupation of Gusii country, took place.

As discussed elsewhere, the establishment of colonial rule over Gusii country was strongly resisted by most Gusii clans, especially the Abagetutu/Kitutu (the largest Gusii clan). When British colonial administrators attempted to invade and over-run Gusii country between 1900 and 1908 they met with stiff and determined resistance from the Gusii warriors. In this resistance, the Gusii were affirming their refusal to accept the establishment of colonial administration in their country. It was only due to the superior British weaponry, accompanied by brutal methods (such as torching homesteads and granaries, and massive carting away of livestock) that led to eventual colonial victory. Most Gusii resisted the colonial invasion and foreign dictation over their country, and over the years developed sophisticated resistance as will be seen later in this book.

When the British Colonial government started

descending upon Gusii, at the start of the 20th century, the Gusii had clearly established themselves in their current homeland. The people had grounded themselves well in terms of social, political and economic development. During this period, as indicated in the previous chapters, the Gusii had managed to fend off external aggression from the warlike Maasai and Kipsigis warriors. They had, over the years, acquired and/or adopted new and more effective military techniques, fighting strategies and weaponry. As a result, they were well prepared in protecting themselves from external aggression. It is also important to note that, following the end of Osaosao War, there was long duration of peace and tranquility in Gusii. This created an ideal enabling environment that allowed the people to engage in various socio-economic initiatives, especially in agriculture and animal husbandry. This resulted in abundant supplies of food and other forms of sustenance resources. Consequently, this social and economic context led to rapid growth of the population of the Gusii.

Due to population increase and the fact that the Gusii were now able to fend off external aggression, various Gusii clans started moving and settling in the existing wider expanses of frontier territory especially in the north eastern and south eastern areas that bordered the Kipsigis and Maasai pastoral communities.

As such, in the period preceding colonial rule, the Gusii were living in an environment of economic success, buttressed by strong military capabilities that had survived several challenges over time. In their fertile territory, the Gusii were living like frontiersmen on the defensive in dispersal and mobile homesteads, and with appropriate and dynamic culture. Their lives were organized around four priorities: food production, tending livestock, military defense, and childbearing. Food production was achieved through shift cultivation of indigenous finger millet, eleusine and sorghum. Milk was obtained from the cattle stock; while meat came the stock of goats and sheep. Aside from being a source of food, livestock was also the currency of the time. It was used in such transactions as dowry payments, compensation required to settle disputes and sacrifices as was necessary.

In the absence of a central authority to govern the group, local defence was necessary in protecting against cattle raids and in performing other military actions. As discussed previously, this required all able-bodied men and the young warriors to be part of the military defence. Furthermore, bearing children was necessary to maintain both food production and defence. The larger the family, the higher the chances that they could feed and defend themselves against attack. Children were also necessary for continuity of lineage.

It is within this broad socio-economic environment, when the Gusii people led relatively prosperous lives that the British colonial administrators started encroaching into Gusii country with an aim of making the region part of the British Protectorate.

Initial contact with the British

The early European explorers, adventure seekers, traders and missionaries who opened East Africa to European influence in the last three decades of the nineteenth century had little contact with or interest in Gusii. This was due, at least in part, to the fact that the Gusii had not practised or been engaged in any long distance trade. Therefore, little impact of the capitalist world economic system had been felt in

Gusii.

The earliest European traveler to the region and the general area was Henry Morton Stanley. He did not, however, enter the Gusii highlands. He merely passed by in the course of his circumnavigation of Lake Victoria in March 1875 as he headed to Buganda. He referred to the area inland from the lakeshore as Ugaya (Ugaia), the name by which the present day districts of South Nyanza and Kisii were known until 1909 (Stanley 1879).

The first European actually to enter Gusii was the German explorer Dr. Fisher in 1900 (Maxon, 1989). No other European seems to have set foot there until the beginning of the colonial period in East Africa. The area inhabited by the Gusii lay well to the south of the normal caravan route from Mombasa at the coast to Uganda, the main focus of British interest in the interior in the late nineteenth century.

With the declaration of a protectorate over Uganda in July 1894, the area to the east of Lake Victoria as far as Naivasha was formally brought under the control of the British. Gusii, though relatively unknown to the British, was thus included in the Eastern Province of the Uganda Protectorate. This province was formally divided into four districts; Mau, Baringo, Suk and Nandi. The Gusii highlands fell within Nandi District: the three divisions of which were Nandi proper, South Kavirondo and Ugaya (Woodward 1902).

Despite the division on a map using a pencil, colonial officials had little direct contact with the Gusii highlands between 1894 and 1902. The closest administrative station to the Gusii highlands was at Kisumu (Matson 1958). The other stations in the Eastern Province were at Nandi, Mumias, Eldama Ravine and Baringo. The influence of the Uganda administration, for the most part, extended only a short distance from the outskirts of the administrative stations. There was little or no trade outside the immediate radius of the stations.

The few British officials stationed in the area were primarily concerned with keeping supply lines open to Uganda. As A. T. Matson (1958) rightly points out, little real administration had been undertaken in the face of the overriding necessity of keeping the Nyando valley clear and construction of the railway up to schedule. The completion of the railway line to Kisumu in 1901, moreover, did not mark any radical change in colonial administration policy.

Nevertheless, it was during the period between 1894 and 1902 when Gusii (the land) was formally included in Uganda's Eastern Province. This was the start of contact between the Gusii and the British. Though no record exists of any British expedition to Gusii before 1902, the Uganda administration was aware of the existence of Gusii. Writing a monograph for the Anthropological Association in 1902, the officer in charge of Eastern Province, C.W. Hobley, (1902) described the "Kisii" as Bantu, and he listed twenty-one divisions of Gusii with their chiefs or headmen. Although this gives an indication that some contact had taken place, much of Hobley's information was not completely accurate. He did not go to the Gusii highlands himself, nor did any of his assistants. Rather, he probably received his information from the Gusii who sought contact with the British or officers in the administrative outposts.

Available historical evidence suggests that it was in fact some Gusii clan leaders (*abakumi*), especially the leader of the smaller Abagisero clan called Ombati, who initiated contact with the British in Kisumu as opposed to the Europeans seeking contacts in

Gusii. According to Gusii folk history, as informed by Gusii elders, the clan was always antagonistic to neighbouring and larger Kitutu unit and hence had decided to strike out on their own trajectory to establish independence from the Kitutu.

The ruler, *omokumi*, of the Abagetutu clan, called Nyakundi, sought to bring back the Abagisero. Nyakundi was powerful and popular. With this 'capital' he attempted to over-run the people of Bogusero. By the middle of the nineteenth century the Abagisero were almost subdued by the powerful leader of the Abagetutu; the latter attacked with viciousness that drove them to seek refuge among their relatives in the adjacent Bonchari region inhabited by the Abanchari.

Realizing that they were in a precarious position, Abagisero sought alternatives. Their leader, Ombati, had few other options other than to seek support from the colonial administrators in Kisumu (Ochieng' 1974). It is said that when the Abagisero heard about the British and their military prowess, they decided to appeal to the new administration for help. To do so, Ombati led a delegation to Kisumu in November, 1900. According to Hobley (1902) Abagisero came on this occasion to seek aid, which he was unable to offer. The Gusii highlands were too far away from the railway line to be of any immediate significance.

Despite the fact that the Uganda administration could not offer any aid, Ombati's appeal to the British was quite significant. Abagisero became the only Gusii clan that was befriended the British and were willing to maintain contacts with the colonialists. From that time on, the British regarded Ombati as an important ally. In fact, he was to serve as an interpreter with the military patrol of 1905 dispatched against the Gusii. As a recognition of his loyalty and friendliness, Ombati was made chief of the Bogusero Location, which owed its existence as a separate entity to British protection.

It was not until the transfer of Eastern Province of Uganda to the East Africa Protectorate, as Kenya was known until 1920, that there were to be closer contacts between the British administration and the Gusii. This transfer took place in March 1902, and the area transferred was soon divided into two provinces, Kisumu and Naivasha. In 1902 and 1903, the colonial administration moved closer to the Gusii with the establishment of administrative posts among neighbouring people. In May 1902, a station was opened among the Kipsigis at Kericho, and in early 1903, a post was established among the Luo at Karungu on the lakeshore (Maxon, 1989). With the establishment of these posts, the Kipsigis and the Luo were brought under British administration and protection. British officials were now in a better position to enter Gusii land and come to closer contact with the Gusii. However, it was not a smooth ride! The first official British attempt to enter Gusii and make contact with the people met with determined and widespread Gusii resistance. For instance, the attempt of another official, F. W. Isaac (the colonial administrator in charge of the outlying post at Karungu in South Nyanza), to enter Gusii in early 1905 was rendered impossible by the widespread resistance of the people (Partington 1905).

Some historians have argued that this failure was not because of any Gusii hostility felt against the British. They posit that it might be because of Gusii relations with their neighbours, especially the Luo, under British protection and control. This, the said historians aver, led to initial conflict between the British and the Gusii (Ochieng' 1974). Looking at the existing situation with hindsight, however, one can state that the existing petty rivalry between the Gusii and the Luo provided a pretext for British intervention in Gusii and the dispatch of a patrol of troops against the Gusii in September 1905. According to G. A. S. Northcote, Assistant Collector (later District Officer) in charge of Karungu, from October 1904 to September 1906, "the Gusii were daily raiding the Kavirondo (Luo) along their borders and were also terrorizing their western neighbours".

We note that this contention of colonial officials was (with high probability) a pretext for attacking the Gusii and subsequently conquer their land. As discussed elsewhere, for hundreds of years, the Gusii had existed in relative political and social harmony with their Luo neighbours, and there was a lot of intercultural exchange among the two groups. Cases of hostile skirmishes between the two groups were rare. Indeed, as noted elsewhere, the Gusii never showed aggression to even the warlike Maasai and Kipsigis. Instead, their war activities were confined to responding to attacks. It is, thus, unlikely that the Gusii were attacking the 'Kavirondo' as Northcote claims (Northcote reference).

Thus, it can be concluded that, in reality, the main objective of the British military expedition into Gusii was to conquer and subdue the Gusii. Towards this end, therefore, the immediate aim of the initial British military expedition was scouting and the selection of a suitable site to establish a colonial administrative post in Gusii (Intelligence Report, 1905). Moreover, establishing an administration post in Gusii had been an aim of the protectorate government for some time. Both Commissioners Sir Charles Eliot and his successor Sir Donald Stewart, wished to see the Gusii brought under British rule (Maxon, 1989). The latter also viewed Gusii as a potential area for European settlement as the region had ideal ecological conditions (cooler temperate-like climate with abundant rainfall and fertile alluvial soils). Following the dispatch of a punitive expedition against the Sotik branch of the Kipsigis living east of the highlands in June of 1905, Stewart wrote to the Colonial Office:

After the Sotik [Kipsigis] have been brought to reason, I hope the Kisii will give no trouble. It is important to open this part of the Protectorate that is well adapted to European settlement... some of the Kisii are friendly and want us to establish a government post in their country, but a large portion of this tribe is inimical and will be likely to give trouble. I have however great hopes that the punishment of the Sotik will bring them to reason (Stewart 1905).

The Colonial Office made no adverse comment on Stewart's plans. It is clear that they concurred with the assessment and the intention expressed in the note. At the conclusion of the operation against the Sotik, Brigadier General Manning, the Inspector General of the King's African Rifles (KAR), commented that expedition should have the effect of keeping the Gusii quiet and that their country was "eminently suited for settlement" (Manning 1905).

Initial Gusii resistance

It was with these motives in mind that in September 1905 a military patrol was dispatched against the Gusii. It was claimed that the intention of the incursion was to obtain compensation for Gusii thefts of 28 livestock belonging to the Luo and the killing of a Luo person under British protection (Intelligence Report 1905). The patrol consisted of one hundred men of V-Company of the 3rd KAR stationed at Kericho. Captain E. V. Jenkins was placed in command of the force, and Northcote was assigned to the patrol as a political officer. Fifty police officers from Kisumu were also ordered to accompany the expedition. The KAR column proceeded west through Kipsigis country to the Sondu River and then south through Luo-inhabited areas. On September 18th, 1905, Jenkins met the rest of his party at Ngozi's village in Luoland just adjacent to the southeastern corner of Gusii. Northcote, fifty policemen, and a doctor now joined the patrol. The political officer had arranged for supplies and interpreters, one of whom was Ombati.

After a day of rest, the patrol entered Gusii on September 20th 1905; it then spent six days, forcibly collecting fines in the South Mugirango area occupied by Abagirango of South Gusii. In every case, the political officer held a *baraza* (public meeting) with clan leaders, *etureti*, and demanded payment of a specified number of cattle as a fine for purported Gusii attacks in Luoland. However, in all parts of the South Mugirango visited by the patrol, promises made in the *barazas* to deliver cattle went unfulfilled. In both instances, September 23rd and 26th, the foreigners started using force in order to collect a sufficient number of cattle and also to "teach the treacherous Kisii tribesmen a lesson" (Jenkins 1905). On the 23rd, the patrol took four hundred head of cattle and on the 26th, one thousand head of cattle were rounded up.

During these military expeditions, Gusii warriors came out to protect their homeland from what was obvious aggression. They put forth determined and widespread resistance. However, charging with their spears and arrows, and coming within very close range, the Gusii suffered heavy casualties from British machine guns. In this clash, many Gusii lost their lives. As well, hundreds of their livestock were captured by the colonial army as a fine for resisting colonial rule (Government Report, 1905). Having experienced the superior military power of the British, the Gusii warriors coined a wily remark: *twakaga ne'risota kani n'omorero* (we thought the enemy had a soft belly; we realize he has fire).

On the 27th of September 1905, the patrol moved into Bonchari territory, where the colonial expedition encountered fierce opposition and resistance. Northcote held a *baraza* to inform the Abanchari on the colonial expedition's arrival and called for cooperation and the payment of fines. However, the Abanchari "were obdurate and refused to pay up" (Jenkins 1905). This perception led to a decision to move forcibly against the Gusii. Perhaps the immediate motive for British to undertake this swift attack on the Abanchari was to subdue the people and capture their valued cattle. According to Gusii accounts, Ombati used this occasion to repay an old score with some of the Abamariba sub-clan of the Abanchari. This pertained to a previous encounter where Abanchari, particularly the Abamariba, had refused to give refuge to Ombati and his Abagisero when the latter we under siege from the Abagetutu. Thus, Ombati urged the British to act more forcefully in order to subdue the belligerent Abanchari.

The following day, 28th of September 1905, the patrol moved out in three columns to forcibly collect cattle, but it faced severe resistance from Abanchari warriors. The Gusii warriors fought very bravely, charging right up to the British soldiers' rifles, forcing one of the columns to fight hand-to-hand with bayonets before the Gusii warriors were repulsed. They seem to have charged so close to the soldiers' bayonets because of lack of familiarity with guns (Jenkins 1905). Jenkins was later told that the warriors believed that the rifles were sticks. Moreover, the Gusii fighting men used spears and arrows that necessitated them to fight at close range. The day's activities cost the Abanchari sixty-seven dead in the field and one hundred and forty wounded whereas the KAR suffered only three casualties. Two thousand heads of cattle were brought in by the patrol.

The battle seemed to the British to have had a salutary impact on the Abanchari and other Gusii clans. Many, including representatives of the Bomachoge, now came forward expressing friendship to the British. On October 2nd, 1905, Northcote held a *baraza* in Bonchari at which five hundred or more attended (Jenkins 1905). He sent a clear message: cooperate and we shall have no more casualties.

Nevertheless, this successful British incursion did not mark the end of Gusii resistance against British occupation. At this stage, the British military expedition had not yet come into contact with the most populous and powerful of the Gusii clans, the Abagetutu, who had previously shown themselves most unfriendly to the British. Ombati also had some scores to settle with the Abagetutu as they represented the greatest threat to his overzealous personal political ambition of creating an independent breakaway group of Abagisero. Not surprisingly, a pitched battle took place in Abagetutu territory. The Abagetutu resisted under the leadership of a wealthy and powerful Gusii *omokumi*, Angwenyi, a grandson of the famous Kitutu leader Nyakundi.

The fighting occurred on October 4th and 5th, 1905 and was the result of what the British termed as 'treacherous behaviour' of the Abagetutu (History of Kisii District, 1907). This behavior was, as Gusii elders of Abagetutu later made clear, the result of conduct on the part of the British that seemed unfair to the Gusii. The British force seized some two hundred head of cattle without the permission of Angwenyi.

This seizure happened after holding what Jenkins termed "a formal peace ceremony" (Jenkins 1905). After the ceremony, Jenkins and his fellow officers felt it 'treacherous' to be attacked while driving the cattle away. Many of the Abagetutu were also offended by the British behaviour of taking their cattle.

The Abagetutu, doubtless to say, were rankled by the fact that one of the principal interpreters for the colonial expedition was Ombati. Seeing a leader of a break-away Abagisero as being a friend of the British was yet another reason for hostility. Ombati lost no time in reminding them that he now had powerful friends, and there was nothing they could do to him. Moreover, he spared no effort in giving the British a bad impression of the Abagetutu.

The fighting that resulted from Abagetutu attempts to take back the cattle on October 4th and 5th, 1905 produced many casualties. By British estimates, ninety-seven Gusii died and twenty-four were wounded, with no loss on the British side (Jenkins 1905). Though the British could look upon the military expedition as a success, many Gusii who were affected recalled the instance with vengeance and bitterness. In this, as in the other incidents previously described, the first contacts between the Gusii and the British left a legacy of resentment. On the same day that the military expedition was being concluded against the Gusii, orders were received to bring the expedition to an end. This is because all available British forces were needed to deal with the impending expedition against the Nandi.

On receiving the orders, British soldiers hurriedly left Gusii to join forces with other British forces to confront the formidable Nandi resistance in the north (Jenkins 1905). It seems that there was apparent concern among the British colonial administrators in Western Kenya that the widely scattered British military forces were being ineffective in countering the determined resistance from the Nandi in the northwest and Gusii in the southwest. At the time of its disbandment, this military expedition had taken over three thousand head of cattle from the Gusii.

The foregoing (reinforcements to subdue the Nandi) is usually given as the reason for the pull back of the British soldiers from their operation in Gusii. However, it is worth noting that at the time the British had not realized their objective of the initial incursion into Gusii. We posit that the determined Gusii resistances against this invasion (in part) made the British soldiers withdraw from Gusii before establishing any effective control over the people. Clearly, this first attempt to subdue the Gusii made the British realize how much they had underrated the resistance they would face.

Due to the prevailing situation, this initial military expedition did not result in the establishment of effective colonial administration in Gusii. Confronted by widespread resistance on two fronts, a southern front in Gusii and the northern front in the Nandi Hills region, the colonial officials had no other option but to withdraw from at least one theatre of operation so that they could concentrate their forces in tackling one front at a time. They chose to withdraw from Gusii. They could not risk defeat from determined Gusii and Nandi fighters (Jenkins 1905). A period of over one year and a half passed before the British would come back and establish their colonial administration over the Gusii.

In reality, colonial administration in Gusii did not begin in earnest until 1907. Early in that year, Northcote and R. W. Hemsted, who had recently been appointed District Commissioner (DC) of Ugaya District[1] visited the Gusii highlands. They chose a site in an area known to the Gusii as Getembe (current Kisii Town) to be the headquarters of their operations in Gusii.

The area lay very close to the borders of the lands inhabited by the clans of Abanyaribari, Abanchari and Abagetutu. It was also fairly centrally located in the Gusii highlands as a whole. The site, moreover, was well supplied with water by two streams (Nyanza Report, 1905-06, PC/ NZA/1/1).

Northcote began to construct the station buildings in February 1907. Although the construction of permanent buildings was not undertaken until May of the same year, it was not long before the new administrative station of Kisii took shape. From April 1st, 1907, Northcote remained in Gusii as the in-charge Assistant District Commissioner. Beginning in May, he initiated the construction of an administrative station on a permanent basis in an elevated area between the two streams. The porters and soldiers who had accompanied the Assistant District Commissioner to the new site did most of the building. They constructed all the buildings with mud walls because of a scarcity of timber (Ongaro 1969).

By July of 1907, significant progress with the station building had been made. Among the first buildings to be constructed were the office for the Assistant District Commission and his house, as well as houses for the porters and the police. A flagpole was erected as well.

The building of an administration station in the Gusii highlands served to open up new forms of economic activity, and Kisii Township was the first centre of these economic operations. The presence of a large

---

1   Gusii was to be included within this District

number of porters engaged in the building created a considerable market for Gusii grain. Salt and cattle were traded to the Gusii in exchange of the grain. Cattle auctions were even held at the new station; payment was usually made in grain. By the time of Dr. Henderson's visit, two shops owned by Indians had opened stores in Kisii (History of Kisii District, KNA: DC/KSI/4/1).

At the same time, as the foundation of Kisii Town and the start of capitalist penetration in the highlands were underway, Northcote was making attempts to establish colonial administration in Gusii as a whole. In 1907 this involved the selection of friendly clan elders as chiefs of the various Gusii clans, implementing the British indirect rule architected by Lord Lugard. These friendly chiefs would act as agents of colonial rule in the everyday life of the people. It also involved building up the authority of those installed as chiefs, and encouraging all people in Gusii to bring criminal and civil cases before the new administration and law enforcement machinery. Finally, laying the foundation of British rule in Gusii involved the beginning of collection of the much hated hut tax. As will be shown later, this colonial administrative process in Gusii was not easy. Most Gusii groups, led by the Abagetutu, were not willing to recognize the British presence nor to accept the orders given by Northcote (Northcote's Diary).

By the end of 1907, Northcote had appointed several chiefs in the Gusii highlands, and the pattern of division of the area into locations based upon recognized clan boundaries was set (these initial locations form the main administrative units in Gusii till today). In addition, the division of the Abagirango into two separate entities (i.e., South Mugirango and North Mugirango) was recognized as Northcote selected separate chiefs for each. Here, it is important to note that Ombati was the first leader to be made chief as a reward for his friendship and collaboration with the British. Ombati was made chief of Abagisero, the very clan he belonged to. It should also be noted that by the end of the year no chief had been picked for the Abagetutu. The persistent resistance of the Abagetutu prevented the selection of a single chief (Nyanza Special Report 1909, KNA; PC/NZA/1/4).

Once chiefs were appointed, Northcote's task was, generally speaking, to oversee the implementation of administrative orders being carried out by the chiefs and headmen. In neither respect was the administration initially successful. The men appointed as chiefs found it very difficult to adapt to the role that the British wanted them to play. They often failed to carry out orders when it would have meant forcing other Gusii to do something the people would resist, such as bring in food for the administration. This type of political coercion was not common in Gusii traditional society, and it took some time before people could adjust to the new concepts of political activity and power that British administration brought.

CHAPTER FIVE

The 1908 resistance

In an attempt to see that its orders were carried out and that cases were brought before them, the colonial administration resorted to the use of force. During the building of the new station, food, firewood and building poles were often in short supply. Chiefs were given explicit orders to bring in these supplies. When these orders were not carried out, coercive means were used in order to get sufficient supplies. For instance, when grain was once in short supply, Northcote gave explicit orders to the chiefs to bring in grain and meat. This order was not obeyed by the people. He responded by personally leading an expedition to outlying Gusii villages and forcibly taking grain, goats and sheep from the people.

The effect of such use of force served only to further alienate large elements of the Gusii, especially the Abagetutu, who had been hostile to the British since 1905. "It appears," wrote Provincial Commissioner John Ainsworth in 1908, "that from the start, the Kitutu people became suspicious of our imposing ourselves upon them". Northcote had, for example, great difficulty in even making contact with any prominent individuals in several parts of Gusii; he found it almost impossible to persuade people to come near him (Ainsworth's Report, 1908).

British attempts to establish their control over the Abagetutu placed them particularly on bad terms with that part of clan responsible for sparking off the armed resistance of 1908 in the Bogeka area. This part of Abagetutu territory had been relatively hard hit by the British military expedition of 1905. It also bordered the Abagisero. Further, the people of Bogeka disliked the British connection with Ombati, the leader of the Abagisero. It was etched in the people's minds that Ombati was person who initially played a role in directing the British soldiers to Gusii. On hearing purported complaints of cattle rustling from Luo living adjacent to Bogeka, Northcote, in June of 1907, went to the area. He found no local elders willing to meet with him. Though he threatened them with reprisals, the people of Bogeka did not bring forward the cattle they were alleged to have stolen from the Luo. The British administrator used absolute force to meet this Abageka hostility and refusal to obey commands. Northcote sent out thirty-five soldiers to recover the cattle regarded as stolen. It was a dawn attack. The soldiers surprised the inhabitants of Bogeka and took nearly one thousand head of cattle. These soldiers were later attacked by Gusii warriors before returning to the Kisii administrative post (Northcote's Diary); at least four of the attackers were killed. This incident served to exacerbate the hatred and dislike which the Gusii had towards the foreign intruders.

With this heightened hatred toward alien aggression in their country, various Gusii clans led by the Abagetutu started to make preparation to declare an all-out war against the occupation. As Gusii customary law demanded during such situations (i.e., when the Gusii are confronted with a common external aggressor) the senior most Gusii leader, *omukumi* Angwenyi of the Abagetutu clan, summoned all the prominent Gusii clan leaders to attend a meeting of *abakumi*. The meeting of *abakumi* was an informal Gusii supreme council whose membership consisted of all prominent leaders from all Gusii clans and sub- clans. This council meeting was held at *Ngoro ya Mwaga* (the

Gusii religious site situated on the Manga Hill referred to earlier in this work) in present-day Central Kitutu location. At this meeting it was agreed by all present that the Gusii were confronting a formidable enemy which required a concerted effort from all Gusii clans to protect their motherland. Without mincing words, Angwenyi advised the Gusii leaders that, unless they all came together as a united entity to confront this formidable enemy, they would all be annihilated by the intruders.

As Gusii customary law on consensus building demanded, Angwenyi made a public proposition asking the leaders present, thus: *mwancheranire ing'a toruanie omosongo* (have you all agreed that we declare war against the white man). Also, as Gusii tradition demanded, all the clan leaders present replied back in unison: *ee twancheranire* (yes, we have all agreed).

Following this solemn proclamation, Angwenyi, assisted by a prominent Gusii priestess Moraa Ng'iti, led the other leaders in taking a magico-religious oath (*emuma*) committing all of them to this agreement. Finally, as custom demanded on such occasions, all the leaders present re-affirmed that "anyone going against this solemn proclamation die" *(tiga onde bwesi okogenda mamincha akue).* This marked the official Gusii declaration of war against the colonial aggressor.

To the Abagetutu, and indeed to the rest of the Gusii, the colonial administrator Northcote epitomized the personification of British aggression over their country; hence, his elimination may have appeared to them to mean an end to alien occupation of Gusii. On his part, Northcote was not unaware of the imminent outbreak of all out resistance against British administration in Gusii. In order to pre-empt this eventuality, in

November 1907, he held a large *baraza* (public meeting) in Kitutu where he warned the Gusii that the colonial administration had taken exception to the hostility which the Gusii were increasingly showing toward the British administration (Northcote's Diary). As a sign of cessation of hostility, he ordered the Gusii to immediately start paying hut tax starting with the Abagetutu. Northcote started enforcing this law in person. Leading an expedition of British soldiers and police, he began hut tax collection in December 1907 in the Bogeka area.

Apart from 'teaching the Gusii a major lesson' for their open hostility toward British rule, the other purpose of this measure was to raise revenue and to stimulate surplus for sale in new capitalist mode of exchange. To promote the latter, the colonial state insisted that the tax be paid in cash, and Gusii men were forced to sell cattle, goats, and sheep in order to obtain money with which to pay the tax. As a result, many Swahili and Somali stock traders were drawn to the district. Any excess money generated could be used for exchange on other goods in the market, effectively triggering off capitalist economic activity.

However, while some Swahili traders were in Bogetutu in early January of 1908, Gusii warriors led by Otenyo ambushed and robbed the traders. When this incident was reported, Northcote decided to investigate (Omwenga 1969). On January 11th, 1908, accompanied by a contingent of KAR soldiers and police, he set out to visit the Abagetutu leader, Angwenyi, to get his assistance in identifying the culprits who had robbed the Swahili traders. He wanted the 'culprits' to face the law. He further ordered that all the inhabitants of Bogetutu should pay a huge fine for the beastly act. However, the Abagetutu openly defied the directive. Northcote then ordered his men to capture cattle to 'teach the local people a lesson' that they will never forget. In the aftermath, Otenyo Nyamaterere, who saw some of his cattle seized by the Europeans, led a contingent of several Abagetutu warriors to lay an ambush for Northcote's caravan and recapture their cattle. Positioning the warriors in strategic locations along the route which Northcorte was using on his way to Getembe administrative post and hiding in the adjacent bushes beside the path, Otenyo personally aimed his spear and struck the official in the back inflicting a severe but not fatal injury.

With the spearing of Northcote, armed resistance was now full blown. Although only wounded, the Assistant District Commissioner was still in great danger. The accompanying police carried him back to Kisii. While recuperating from the near-fatal wound inflicted upon him by Otenyo, Northcote sent two police officers to the provincial headquarters at Kisumu. He also sent a report of the attack to the district headquarters at Karungu (Ongaro 1969).

The day following the attack on Northcote was a crucial one for the colonial administration in Gusii. Once the Gusii warriors found out that Northcote was not dead, they took up arms and proceeded to Getembe in full force, to 'finish the Job' (Ongaro 1969). Around noon on the 12th, they gathered on the hills surrounding Kisii. Barbed wire had already been laid down around the *boma*; Northcote now armed all men who knew how to use a riffle, including prisoners from the jail, to take defensive positions and defend the administrative post. He then collected all the women and porters, traders, and servants in Kisii around his house (Northcote's Diary). This made an imposing looking force of some three hundred people. Most of them were unarmed. The sight of all the people, however, was enough to keep these Gusii warriors from attempting to attack. Many of them had learned in 1905 the folly of attacking a force armed with rifles. Consequently, they withdrew from the vicinity of the station.

Although they did not assault the colonial post, the Gusii warriors went ahead to attack the Abagisero and other smaller sub-clans that were thought to have associated with colonial rule and whose protection the British seemed no longer able to guarantee. Twenty policemen were killed in the days following the spear-attack. A trader of Indian descent and two porters from Luo land were also slain.

Thus the spearing of Northcote sparked off an open second wave of Gusii resistance against colonial rule; the Gusii rose up in arms to protest arbitrary acts on the part of the British in the course of their attempts to establish their rule in all parts of the highlands. Furthermore, there was extreme uneasiness among most Gusii people about the new system of exchange that carried with it the probable insistence on new modes of capitalistic production.

The spearing of Northcote, the killing of the twenty policemen, the murder of Luo porters, the killing of an Indian trader as well as the attacks on the Abagisero clan became a great concern to the government of the East Africa Protectorate. Attacks on Abagisero clan took place on 12th and 13th January, 1908 and it was these in particular which convinced the government that strong punitive action was called for. John Ainsworth, a veteran colonial administrator in the protectorate, received Northcote's letter on the 12th of January, 1908. He immediately sent a doctor to attend to the wounded official.

On the 14th of January, Ainsworth received information on the events of the 12th and 13th which he termed a "general rising.... against the government" (Ainsworth's Report). He, therefore, initiated more severe measures. The Assistant Superintendent of Police at Kisumu, Robert Foran, was sent with all available police to Kisii. Foran set off on the same day with fifty-two men (Foran 1936). Ainsworth also ordered the 5th KAR at Lumbwa to send fifty men to Kisii station. At the same time, the PC wired the governor reporting further hostilities. It was this telegram, which led to the dispatch of a full-scale punitive expedition against the Gusii.

The Government quickly set in motion the steps necessary for the assembling of such an expedition. A meeting of the Executive Council on the 15th of January sanctioned the dispatch of troops under the command of Lt. Colonel J. D. Mackay (Executive Council 1908). Mobilization orders were quickly issued. The bulk of the troops to be used were on cattle duty in the Athi River area east of Nairobi. These were moved to Nairobi and travelled by special train to Kisumu on the 17th of January. Ainsworth had been instructed to provide fifty Nandi levies to join the force as well as a large number of porters.

On the 14th, R. W. Hemsted arrived from Karungu. Three days later, Foran arrived with the doctor who, fearful of the Abagetutu, had been waiting in the Luo location of Mumbo. On the 18th, fifty men of the KAR arrived from Lumbwa via Kisumu (Northcote's Diary). During this same period, the punitive expedition was making its way to Gusii country. It was made up of forty British officers, 327 NCO and men, a doctor, fifty Nandi levies, and some five hundred porters (Ainsworth's Report). This force reached Kisumu by the 18th, and proceeded by lake to Kendu Bay on the 19th. Here a base camp was established, and after Ainsworth had joined the expedition, it began its march towards the highlands on 21st of January. The British force made its entrance into Gusii territory on the morning of 22nd of January.

On entering Gusii, the expedition mercilessly began capturing cattle, burning homes, and killing anyone on sight as the troops proceeded towards Kisii station. Mackay divided his force into three columns, covering a frontage of about ten miles; he then proceeded to drive any Gusii in the area in front of him towards the station. Taken completely by surprise, the Gusii suffered heavily from this day's operations. Huge numbers of livestock were captured by the invading force, many houses and cattle enclosures burnt, and some hundred men, according to British estimates, killed. According to information received from Gusii elders, however, over five hundred Gusii were massacred and thousands of cattle were captured (Mackay's Report 1908).

Realizing the folly of confronting the machine gun power of the invader, the Gusii started to wage sporadic hit and run attacks (guerilla warfare) to defend their villages and their valued herds. The British took stock in the hope that this might bring the Gusii to battle. "I have found from years of experience in this country," wrote Mackay in his official report, "that the native will never fight or be brought to action until his flocks and herds are laid hands on." (Mackay's Report) Although this practice did not result in a pitched battle with the Gusii, the tactic seems to have had, according to both British and Gusii elders' accounts, the effect of demoralizing the Gusii. They did not make any effort to disrupt the march of the expedition after this.

The colonial military expedition went ahead to cause terror in the whole of Gusii, burning houses, killing anyone on sight and capturing livestock. Although these operations were a great success from the point of view of Ainsworth and Mackay, not all the officials agreed with such assessment of triumph.

The all out destruction incensed Northcote, who bore no ill will against the Gusii, so much so that later in a letter to his father in England he bitterly observed: "it would take too long to describe the absolute idiocy, obstinacy, and want of knowledge of military operations in this country which they showed" (Northcote to his father, 12th February 1908, DC/KSI/4/1). Northcote's complaints and advice went largely unheeded. The expedition continued on the note it had begun, capturing cattle, burning houses, and shooting all those who interfered with it, showing precious little consideration for Gusii lives and property. C. Ojwando Abuor (1971) has described it as "one of the most hateful operations under which the Kenya Africans endured".

The punitive expedition went on with its operation in the face of little organized opposition from the Gusii. The troops reached the station on January 23rd 1908; they camped in Bogeka, near the present day Nyakoe market some five miles from Kisii Town, and remained there through the 25th of January, sending out patrols into western Kitutu to capture cattle. Fifty two Abagetutu, according to official British estimates, were killed in the course of these operations with no loss on the British side (Mackay's Report).

CHAPTER SIX

Prelude to colonial rule

Subduing the Gusii

Despite the fact that there were pitched battles fought, wanton destruction of property and huge fatalities suffered by the Gusii people does provide a telling commentary on colonial misrule and oppression. It is little wonder that those in the colonial headquarters in Britain ended up viewing these military expeditions as butchery. Hundreds of Gusii men were driven from their homes and forced to take refuge in the bush for several weeks in order to escape death and save their herds (Ongaro 1969). On the 26th of January, the expedition moved up the Manga escarpment on the northeast of the Getembe station (the epicenter of Abagetutu resistance). It was on this occasion that Ainsworth received his first indication that the Abagetutu desired an end to hostilities (Ainsworth's Report). In this mission, Ainsworth was the Chief Political Officer and one who had been bestowed the responsibility of deciding when the expedition had achieved its objective of subduing the Abagetutu.

The Abagetutu leader, Angwenyi, came to Ainsworth to ask for cessation of hostilities between the Gusii and the colonial administration. However, this did not mean an end to the fighting. Hearing that some Abagetutu cattle had been driven into North Mugirango, the expedition proceeded through Bogetutu to the home of Chief Ndubi. He handed over the cattle to the British, but the march to North Mogirango was not a peaceful one as ninety-eight Kitutu were killed on the way.

While at Ndubi's camp, all captured cattle were sent under escort to Kericho. The expedition remained in North Mugirango until the 2nd of February.

Nevertheless, pressure for peace was by now mounting, as the Abagetutu clearly desired the operations to be brought to a close. After his initial meeting with Angwenyi, Ainsworth met with him and their followers in the next two days. These meetings were satisfactory from the administration's point of view. On the 28th of January Angwenyi accompanied with other Abagetutu leaders came to Ainsworth's camp with food and a portion of their hut tax (Ainsworth's Report). Angwenyi further showed his desire for an end to hostilities and an improvement in relations with the British by bringing Otenyo, the man who had speared Northcote, to the station on the 1st of February. This was as had been demanded by the colonial administrators. When Otenyo presented himself to the colonial administrators as demanded, he was put in custody and eventually beheaded by the administrators. Also as per the assertion of Gisii elders, the head of Otenyo and his war-paraphernalia were shipped to the UK where they were stored in a national museum.

On February 4th, Angwenyi informed Ainsworth, who was now once more at Kisii station, that all Abagetutu sub-clans desired peace. Although he had resisted the British in 1905 and had earlier called for action against the current forces, Angwenyi was now ready to actively collaborate as a means of saving his people from massacre at the hands of the superior military power of the British. The following day, Ainsworth officially informed Mackay that the expedition could be terminated. "I have the honour to inform you" he wrote, "that I consider the revolted Kisii have now been punished, and consequently...I have to inform you that active operation may be brought to a close" (Ainsworth's Report). In a second letter, Ainsworth further commented:

> On termination of hostilities in Kisii country and in continuation of my letter of this date, I have the honour to inform you that in my opinion the expedition has achieved the object for which it was mobilized. The Kitutu section of the Kisii tribe has been utterly demoralized and has been taught a most severe lesson. Undoubtedly the prestige of the government has been maintained in a most striking manner (Ainsworth's Report).

At the same time that the Gusii were expressing a desire for an end to military operations, so too was the Colonial Office in London. This was especially so after the reception of a telegram of January 31st from Governor Sir James Hayes Sadler listing Gusii casualties at more than one hundred killed with no loss on the British side (Sadler to Elgin, telegram, 31 January 1908, C.O. 533/41). On reading the telegram, Winston Churchill, then Under-Secretary of State for the Colonies, minuted:

> I do not like the tone of these reports. No doubt the clans should have been punished, but 160 have now been killed *outright without any further casualties* on our side.... It all looks like butchery. If the H. of C. gets hold of it, all our plans in E.A.P. [East African Protectorate] will be under a cloud. Surely it cannot be necessary to go on killing these defenseless people on such enormous scale (Minute by Churchill, 3 February 1908, on Sadler to Elgin, telegram, 31 January 1908, C.O. 533/41).

As a result of Churchill's intense feelings, a telegram with a strong message was sent to the governor on February 3rd, which expressed London's regret at the large number of the Gusii killed. The telegram urged Governor Sadler to confine the bloodshed to very narrow limits.

> "Impress immediately upon the O/C," the telegram went on, "that every effort should be made to induce the enemy to submit peacefully after the most severe lesson they have received, and mercy should at once be extended to all not personally concerned in the original outbreaks" (Elgin to Sadler, telegram, 3 February 1908, C.O. 533/41).

This message did not reach the commander in the field until February 6th, after hostilities had ceased. Nevertheless, the regret expressed over the large numbers of Gusii killed served to dampen the martial ardor of Mackay's staff. Tellingly, they were awarded no medals for the campaign in Gusii.

With the end of punitive operations, the main body of troops was withdrawn and a settlement made with the Abagetutu. Most of the soldiers arrived back in Nairobi on February 11th. A full company was, however, left in Gusii; it remained there until September. A large *baraza* attended by most leading elders of the Abagetutu was held on February 12th. At this meeting, the British made Angwenyi the chief of what was now termed Kitutu location. The chieftaincy was to remain in Angwenyi's family down to the post–colonial era. It was not hard to see why he was appointed as chief since he was the most prominent Abagetutu leader, *omokumi,* before the arrival of the British.

Furthermore, it was Angwenyi himself who led his people to seek a cessation of hostilities with the British after realizing that their spears and arrows were no match to British gun power. With the crushing of Abagetutu resistance in 1908, the colonial administrative system established among the other Gusii clans and sub-clans now began to function among the Abagetutu as well. In addition, with the appointment of a single chief, the collection of hut tax, and the submission of disputes to the administration for settlement, the largest Gusii clan finally came, despite the earlier armed resistance, under British rule. It marked the close of a chapter in British rule in the Gusii highlands. Now established colonial domination would never be so openly and forcefully challenged again. The suppression of the resistance clearly indicated the fruitlessness of force. Nevertheless, the events of 1908 cannot be viewed in an entirely negative light.

Despite their heavy punishment, persistent Gusii resistance to colonial rule seems to have put off any ideas of alienating parts of the highlands for European settlement out of the minds of British officials. The hopes of Stewart in that regard were never voiced again after 1908. Consequently, Gusii resistance to colonial rule did produce what must be seen as the positive effect of "saving" the Gusii from losing land to white settlers. Although, the Gusii would continue to manifest resistance in different forms in the years that followed, still the events of 1908 did bring about conditions conducive for accommodation of the bulk of the Gusii population within the new colonial order.

The end of the war

It is important to state that the Gusii warriors demonstrated great bravery and courage in their encounter with the British colonial soldiers, sometimes charging, fiercely, towards the enemy notwithstanding the emanating hail of gun fire. In this regard, coming within very close range, the Gusii warriors could engage the enemy in face-to-face combat, sometimes forcing the British soldiers to use bayonets instead of shooting directly at the warriors. And all the youthful and energetic Gusii warriors had were sharpened spears and a determination to defeat occupation that fueled the resistance.

It should be restated that, as tradition demanded, the Gusii warriors were not prepared to suffer defeat. They were not ready to face humiliation and ridicule as the people whose generation allowed an external enemy to vanquish the Gusii community and/or take over their homeland. Consequently, the warriors were emotionally and psychologically prepared to die defending their homeland against the enemy occupation. This was deeply ingrained in their psyches through various rites of passage, particularly the circumcision rituals. As presented in other sections of this work, these cardinal rituals were avenues of inculcating into the Gusii youthful males a strong sense of community and the readiness to fight to the last man in defence of one's family, clan and indeed the whole Gusii community. This preparedness was essential in responding against any form of internal and external aggression.

The warriors lived to these expectations in encountering the British. However, it was only after the Gusii elders realized that they were on the verge of losing a whole generation of male youths, livestock and their homes that they issued a directive for cessation of hostilities. In this respect, the warriors were ordered to stop waging war against the British. Woe unto him that defied the directive from the elders as they would be cursed. In fact the elders had pronounced a curse against any Gusii youth who, in one way or the other, went against this momentous directive.

Thus we postulate that the main factor that contributed to the eventual defeat and conquest of the

Gusii by the British soldiers, as was the case with most other African resistance movements in different parts of the continent, was the inferior weaponry that was used by the warriors compared to that of the colonizers. Due to technological advancement, especially in the production of military and other related hardware, the British had far superior weaponry compared to that of the Gusii. This superior weaponry included machine guns, magazine guns, bullets and gun powder that was substantially lethal compared with the bows, arrows, spears and shields used by the Gusii. Thus as much as the Gusii warriors waged a determined resistance to the British colonizers in the long run they were bound to be defeated.

CHAPTER SEVEN

Other forms of Gusii resistance

After the military conquest of the Gusii by the British colonial government, the British administration started putting in place punitive measures aimed at containing the Gusii people. These actions were two pronged, targeting Gusii young men and livestock.

The British forcefully captured Gusii young men and took them to work as labourers. The young people were deployed in the construction of roads while others worked in European settler farms, and later on served as War Corp Carriers and soldiers in the King's African Rifles (KAR). In addition, the colonial administrators captured thousands of Gusii livestock (Maxon, 1989).

However, as much as the Gusii had been vanquished militarily by the superior weaponry of the colonial army, they did not immediately give in to colonial rule and/or colonial control over their much cherished homeland. Thus, having undergone extreme suffering, including destruction/loss of property, rape and high levels of fatalities, the Gusii turned inwards to their cultural values and beliefs to counter what they perceived as a major socio-political and economic catastrophe that had befallen them as a people (Ongaro, 1969). In particular, the people turned to the teachings of their heroes of yonder as a form of solace and re-orientation to the new realities that were confronting them as a society. Within this broad socio-cultural context, the teachings of the renowned Gusii prophet Sakagwa Ng'iti, became pertinent to the situation which the Gusii were confronting.

According to Gusii cultural-religious psyche, many of the prophecies of Sakagwa had been fulfilled based on what had and/or was happening to the community (Ongaro, 1969; Maxon, 1989). The prophecies included the accurate predictions on the arrival and eventual establishment of colonial rule over the Gusii, the construction of the Kenya-Uganda railway and the emergence of Getembe (the current Kisii Town) as a major urban centre.

Furthermore, the mysteries surrounding the death of Sakagwa strengthened the beliefs of the Gusii people in his prophecies. According to Gusii mythology, Sakagwa had not suffered natural death. He had just vanished to the 'other world', leaving behind his noticeable traditional regalia including his mystical stool, spear and walking stick. Indeed, according to Gusii folk history, there is no identifiable grave where Sakagwa was buried. Hence, the prophet must have disappeared to the 'yonder', carried by supernatural powers. More interestingly, Sakagwa had not only prophesized about the coming of the Europeans and the subsequent Gusii resistance, he had also prophesized that the Europeans will leave and/or vacate Gusii one day.

We postulate that the widespread acceptance by the Gusii people of Sakagwa prophecies greatly contributed to the emergence of traditional religious movement called *Enyamumbo*. The teachings of *Enyamumbo* were, completely, at variance with the principles of Christianity as enunciated by the European missionaries who were trying to establish their base in Gusii. In particular, the indigenous religion taught the Gusii people to have trust in their departed ancestors who they believed will always intercede to the Gusii Supreme Being, *Engoro* on their behalf in all matters. Consequently, as per the beliefs of the Gusii people, ancestor intercession was critical to making the people overcome the major catastrophe that had befallen them due to the establishment of the British colonial rule. *Enyamumbo* 'personified' these beliefs. In this regard, the main religious rhyme that was sung during the *Enyamumbo* worship was basically requesting *Engoro* to intercede and banish the colonial rulers from the Gusii homeland:

The Enyamumbo Religious Song	
Sabaye, Sabaye, Sabaye!!	Ullah, Ullah, Ullah!!
Tata okure ogocha moyo !!	Our ancestors who had died have risen
na baba okure ogocha moyo!! x2	Again!! x2
Risosu riiruruke!!	Let the Europeans be vanquished!!

For the Gusii, an opportunity to chase away the British from their homeland arose in September, 1914 specifically at the start of World War I. This is when German soldiers, crossing from Tanganyika in a coordinated attack on the British establishments in Kenya, attacked and overran the British defense stations in Kisii Town. In the process, the Germans literary ran the British out of Kisii town. To the Gusii, it was an indication of Sakagwa being vindicated. It was the fulfilment of his prophecies.

During the attack by the Germans, the Gusii people watched with disbelieve the evolving situation where whites and/or Europeans were fighting each other over presumed control of Gusii. The Gusii, particularly from the Kitutu and Nyaribari clans, neighbouring Kisii Town, gathered in the adjacent hills to watch with bemusement the unfolding events (Maxon, 1989).

As much as the German soldiers had overran and expelled the British from Kisii Town, they did not attempt to occupy the town (Omwenga, 1969). The place was now vacated by the white foreigners. Realizing that both the Germans and the British soldiers had departed, a large number of Gusii people converged in the town. With a lot of enthusiasm, they ransacked the place carrying away most of the movable assets that they could find. In particular, they looted all household and office goods. They also destroyed most of the buildings put up by the British in the town (Ongaro, 1969).

However, things took a turn soon. At the beginning of 1915, the British Colonial Administration mobilized reinforcements from Kisumu and Kendu Bay administrative posts to confront the German soldiers in Kisii Town. But, when the British soldiers arrived in Kisii, they found that the Germans had already withdrawn from the town and, as a consequence, the British easily re-captured the town much to the consternation of the Gusii.

Immediately the British colonial administrators re-occupied Kisii town, they started the process of reasserting themselves. First, they turned their attention to instilling maximum punishment to the people perceived as being responsible for the destruction of the town. The Colonial District Commissioner (DC), Spencer gathered all the appointed colonial chiefs and headmen and gave them a dressing-down for failing to prevent their people from looting and/or destroying the town. Most of the chiefs present informed Spencer that, it was, majorly, the people of Kitutu, Nyaribari and Bonchari who were responsible for the looting and destruction (Maxon, 1989).

This is the information that the DC wanted to set things in motion and he promptly embarked on action. He ordered that all young men from the three named clans be seized and made to return the stolen property. The young men were seized, however, no stolen goods were recovered. When this happened, the seized victims were summarily executed by firing squad in broad daylight and clear view of a large number of assembled Gusii chiefs, headmen and elders ostensibly as a measure of teaching 'treacherous Gusii tribesmen' a lesson that they will never forget. The Gusii youths who were killed by the colonial administration (numbering over 2000) were buried in unmarked mass graves around Kisii Town (Ongaro, 1969).

Worse still, more punitive measures were mooted and undertaken against the Gusii especially for those from the Kitutu, Nyaribari and Bonchari clans. Their houses were burned en-mass, women were raped with abandon and over 40,000 head of cattle were seized during the operation (Maxon, 1989). In addition, there were many fatalities.

Furthermore, more than 10,000 young men were captured and forced to work in the reconstruction of Kisii Town. The people were also ordered to bring all their weaponry (spears, shields and other war paraphernalia) which were destroyed in a huge bonfire witnessed by the assembled Gusii elders.

Consequently, it should be noted that, the Gusii people realized that it was futile to resist (in conventional terms) and/or wage war against the British colonial government given the suffering they had faced. The colonialists had by far more superior weaponry and other forces of imperial coercion. However, as already presented above, immediately the Gusii suffered this major defeat from the colonialists, the people changed tactics. They resorted to other forms of covert and overt resistance. It should be noted that much of these latter forms of coverts and overt resistance do not form part of this book; we only allude to some at a very limited scale here.

The other forms of resistance mooted by the Gusii following their defeat in the hands of the British included refusing to co-operate fully with the colonial administration's policies and governance systems. These actions included resistance to the introduction of cash crops and refusing to pay hut and poll taxes. The Gusii figured out, correctly, that the administration wanted cash crops as a means of raising exports from the colony. They also understood that taxes paid went to support the colonial administration. In this respect, therefore, and without facing the colonialists with arms and confrontation, the Gusii were able to impact the administration, hitting it where it hurt! The administration failed to meet both cash crop production and tax collection targets.

Thus, it should be noted that these forms of resistance and other types of reactions to British colonial rule were, in the long-run, critical in making the colonial administration moderate some of their imperial initiatives that were unpopular with the Gusii populace. Thus, even after losing the war against the British soldiers and experiencing a lot of suffering, the Gusii did not become passive receptors of colonial conceptions and policies.

Clearly the various forms of Gusii resistance against colonial rule (both overt and covert forms of resistance) had some impact on the subsequent direction and the forms of administrative laws and governance policies that were adopted by the colonial government.

Therefore, it can be articulated that as much as the Gusii were defeated militarily, their intense resistance against colonial rule had some impacts in the manner in which the colonial administrators governed Gusii.

In summary, some of the impacts included the British changing tactic, in the manner in which they administered Gusii and encouraged rapid spread of Christianity as a means of pacifying the Gusii; being cautious not to annex Gusii land for European settlement and; entrenching clanism among the Gusii as a means of dividing and controlling the people. Also fearing that the 'belligerent Gusii tribesmen' might rebel again, the British administrators resorted to holding constant *barazas* that were aimed at hoodwinking the Gusii into accepting colonial administration.

CHAPTER EIGHT

Conclusion

Overview

This book provides some background on the Gusii, and a systematic presentation of the various survival strategies and military techniques that the Gusii had developed and used, over many years. These strategies and techniques enabled the group to survive man-made and natural calamities and other challenges that they faced from time to time. Surrounded by non-Bantu, and hostile communities such as the Maasai and Kipsigis, the Gusii had over the years developed various defensive and other forms of survival systems that, in the long-run, enabled them fend off of internal and external aggression. These methods of self-preservation were also at the core of the Gusii identity. Within that given context, the book also provides an enunciation of Gusii resistance to the establishment of colonial rule over their homeland.

In this regard, when British colonial soldiers ventured into Gusii at the beginning of the twentieth century, the Gusii were experiencing relative peace and tranquility, and overall socio- economic development. This is a period that followed their success in fending off external aggression from the surrounding hostile communities. Consequently, when the Kings African Rival (KAR) soldiers started making inroads into Gusii with the aim of subduing and/or coercing the Gusii into accepting colonial rule, they were met with determined and persistent resistance from Gusii warriors. It is worth noting that, initially, the Gusii warriors were able to stand their ground in defence of their homeland despite incurring heavy losses. They were, however, defeated once the colonial forces regrouped to attack with abandon, causing wanton destruction in the process. Gusii elders, fearing extermination of their people, had to call off the resistance. Clearly, the use of superior weaponry enabled the British soldiers to defeat the Gusii. This defeat led to colonial occupational of Gusii, which had long-lasting impact, experienced to date. On the other hand, the resistance could have been at the centre of the decision by the British not to alienate land in Gusii for occupation as had been intended. In this section we articulate the main social, economic and political consequences of colonial rule over the Gusii.

Destruction of Gusii governance and administration systems

The conquest and eventual establishment of colonial rule over the Gusii triggered a critical process of social, economic, cultural and political transformation of the community. To start with, following the conquest, the Gusii indigenous cultural values and social norms came under siege. There was covert and overt coercion, on the people to abandon these time-tested practices in favour of European and alien social, political and cultural values.

In particular, the people found themselves abruptly enmeshed into Western cultural values and 'philosophies', with materialism at their core. Further, the defeat inflicted lasting damage on the community's collective psyche. Inadvertently, the people started to believe that their indigenous cultural heritage and communal practices were inferior vis-à-vis those of their new rulers.

It should be noted that, prior to the arrival of the British, the Gusii, as is the case with most other indigenous African communities, had relatively well-articulated indigenous systems of governance, and the administration of law and order. In Gusii, these indigenous institutions were based on the principle of bottom-up approach. Governance started from the smallest socio-cultural unit, the homestead (*omochie*), extending to the village level or clan (*etureti*) and eventually spread to the topmost organ of indigenous governance and administration of justice (*abakumi*) (Akama, 2017). Specifically, these indigenous institutions took care of most aspects of administration and maintenance of law and order. For instance in aspects of administration of justice, the *abakumi* court was at the apex of Gusii jurisprudence. This body handled intricate and/or precedent-setting cases affecting the whole community. These were matters such as unresolved murder and witchcraft cases, protracted land disputes involving two and more families, and intractable inter-clan disputes.

More importantly, the Gusii indigenous legal systems were based on egalitarian principles of equity, consensus-building, reconciliation, restitution and natural justice. The main aim of the administration of justice, in Gusii indigenous systems, was to promote peace and harmony in society, within families, among clans and across the whole of the Gusii community. Unlike Western and/or European jurisprudence systems, the indigenous legal systems were neither retributive nor adversarial in nature. This was also consistent with the Gusii belief system that linked any potential punishment to potential harm via the wrath of ancestral spirits and *Engoro*.

With the conquest and final establishment of British colonial rule over the Gusii, these indigenous systems of governance and the administration of justice were almost fatally disrupted. A case in point is the principle of *chinsoni*, which governed the society's individual behaviour and social relations. Its destruction meant the whole orientation of Gusii lifestyle was torn asunder. *Chinsoni* offered a social structure that offered predictable ways of interaction between people of different relations and status. The order that resulted from this time-tested fell apart as a consequence of its destruction. Over many years, the Gusii cultural values, indigenous social fabric, and structures of governance had held the people together and accorded meaningful to life and made it worth living. The obliteration of these attributes led to severe and far-reaching negative social, economic and cultural consequences.

Most of these consequences are still being felt among the Gusii today. For instance, in traditional society there was utmost respect for elders. They had moral authority as the custodians of the Gusii communal information, knowledge, skills, and competencies. With the colonial order and its Christianity accompaniment, these indigenous systems were destroyed with the attendant negative consequences. The consequences include the break-down of law and order in the whole community, family disintegration, and increased criminal incidents such arson, theft, rape, incest and general violence. We posit that this arose, in part, from the accumulation of many unresolved cases that the new system could not deal with. These daunting administrative and legal issues are challenges that still confront the Gusii and other indigenous African communities in the contemporary society.

At the advent of colonialism, Gusii indigenous social fabric held the community together. Indigenous governance and legal systems handled sensitive and, in many respects, emotive cases involving intricate issues, such as witchcraft, murder, rape and land disputes. In the wake of destruction of these indigenous institutions and structures, aggrieved parties started taking the law into their own hands. In the process, some could take liberty to settle scores and/or wrongs committed against them (as individuals or groups) whether real and/or imagined. Perhaps taking a cue from the way the Gusii resistance was crushed, might and use of force against perceived opponents became entrenched, something that was unheard of in traditional society. The result was a rise in incidents of extreme violence, regardless of consequences, to resolve disputes and/or subdue adversaries. With the establishment of British colonial rule in Gusii, cases of arson and murder became rampant. This is in addition to incidents of regular infighting and scuffles amongst opposed parties over issues concerning land. With dwindling land sizes, such disputes have become even more vicious, especially among immediate family members with the attendant far-reaching negative consequences of fatalities, injuries, and wanton destruction of property; and let alone the negative impact on family relations. Indeed, we continue to witness this same social behaviour and negative attitudes in most parts of Gusii, other parts of Kenya and the whole of the African continent. It is fair to conclude that the destruction of indigenous systems of political governance and administration of justice left a major gap that has not been filled with the Western systems.

Disbandment of Youth Encampments (*Ebisarate*)

With the conquest of the Gusii, top-down systems of colonial administration and law enforcement were established. Inevitably, Gusii indigenous order and systems were destroyed. One such casualty is the institution of *ebisarate*. Typically, *ebisarate* were encampments that were situated in strategic geographical locations throughout Gusii land where all able-bodied young men from the same lineage or clan lived together under the watch of older men. As discussed elsewhere, *ebisarate* served both military and cultural purposes. With the advent of colonial rule, however, *ebisarate* were criminalized and forcefully disbanded. As explained elsewhere, one of the cardinal duties of the youths in the encampments was to protect the community against external aggression. In addition, it was in the encampments that livestock, especially cattle, from different homesteads that belonged to the same kinship, were kept for security reasons. The youth kept vigil over the livestock, especially at night when the enemy and/ or cattle rustlers were likely to attack.

With the disbandment of *ebisarate,* however, this well-organized social and administrative system of keeping energetic youth in productive communal initiatives, and call to duty, disappeared overnight. No form of alternative strategy of engaging the young men replaced the system. As a consequence, from this time onwards, the youths were mostly left on their own loitering in village markets and pathways. As a result, they became prone to various forms of anti-social and/or criminal behaviour. These formerly engaged youth became perpetrators of incidents of petty crime, thuggery, rape, and other family scuffles. These forms of anti-social behaviour and security related challenges are increasingly witnessed in many parts of present day rural Gusii. This is notwithstanding the fact that there exist modern national and county structures of governance and law enforcement systems.

Accelerated population growth in Gusii

In traditional Gusii society, as discussed elsewhere, young people followed a specific path to adulthood. Once initiated, young men spent a fair amount of time maturing. Indeed, most Gusii young men were only allowed to marry after spending 3 to 5 years in the *ebisarate*, and, by the time they graduated and hence qualified to leave *ebisarate*, they were usually above the age of 25 years. As such, most of the youth entered marriage during their late stages of growth, in their late 20s up to the mid-30s. With the disruption of established order and disbandment of *ebisarate*, the young men started staying home with their parents. In most instances, they had no major obligations imposed upon them. In the long-run, most of them started marrying at a very young age.

The disbandment of the military encampments left a large cohort of young men ready to jump into marriage. The net effect of this situation was the severe shortage of livestock in most families that could be used to pay bride wealth. In the evolving situation, new forms of marriage arrangements emerged that were at variance with the strict regulations and procedures that governed a Gusii customary marriage. For instance, girls at the tender age of as low as fifteen (15) years started to elope with relatively young men who were also in their teens. These forms of marriages were usually initiated by the young couples, without the consent of their parents and/or without the payment of the requisite bride wealth. Consequently, these very young couples started giving birth to children at a very early age. These forms of early marriage exposed the women to situations of giving birth to too many children, sometimes as many as twelve per woman!

In addition, with the changing circumstances, many parents also started circumcising their children at a very early age, as low as eight years. According to Gusii tradition, any young girl who had gone through initiation was considered ready for marriage. As a result, most young girls started to get married at a very tender age, thus enhancing the possibility of having many children before reaching menopause. All these factors created a situation of unprecedented population growth among the Gusii.

Clearly, the abrupt interruption and disappearance of indigenous institutions of governance and indigenous social control mechanisms triggered the process of a unique demographic phenomenon of exponential growth of the Gusii population. For instance, with the weakening of the indigenous code of conduct concept, *chinsoni,* that provided specific rules and regulations on how people belonging to the opposite gender and different age groups were supposed to relate to one another, people could engage in sexual relationships that were hitherto forbidden. These manifested themselves in things such as engagement in wantonness sexual activities, especially among the youth, increased incidents of unauthorized early marriages with the attendant unplanned pregnancies and child birth. In some cases, young people of the same clan could engage in sexual relationships, something that was a taboo in traditional society as clan members were viewed as a family.

Inevitably early marriages and wanton sexual activities (even among unmarried couples) contributed to high rate of population growth, more so because now women had a longer child-bearing duration having started the process at a tender age. The attendant social and economic consequences of all this superfluous sexual behaviour, and other forms of anti-social activities, are quite obvious and have had far reaching impacts on the life and social wellbeing of the Gusii. For instance, within a very short time span (1920-1980) Gusii population increased from a paltry 150,000 people to over 1.5 million people. Currently, the Gusii population is estimated to be over 3.5 million people. In a very short timeframe of less than 70 years, the Gusii population has increased more than tenfold. This is an unprecedented demographic phenomenon even with respect to global trends. However, it can also be argued that, in recent years, with the advent of Western medicine, infant mortality rate has reduced drastically. At the same time, maternal health has also improved, thus reducing the number of women and children who could possibly die at childbirth due to poor access to health care.

Last but not least, the study of the Gusii community provides a very good case study of how the phenomena of European imperialism in general, and British colonialism in particular, transformed the socio-economic, cultural and political orientation of African communities. Using their military might and the strategy of divide and rule, which was perfected by the British, the colonizers were able to impose their governance and exploitative economic systems on African communities. As such, the African communities were forcefully linked to the European capitalistic systems as peripheral territories that provided raw materials and markets for the Western world. On the other hand, the conquest and eventual establishment of colonial rule on African communities such as the Gusii had far-reaching negative consequences on the communities. These consequences reverberate to date. On the other hand, for factors that are outside the scope of this study, African communities have not had a response to the external conquest and its impact on their societies. African communities have not played their fundamental role in resolving these negative impacts and as such this argument is double sided.

REFERENCES

Abuor, C. Ojwando. 1971. *White Highlands No More.* Nairobi: Pan African Researchers.

Ainsworth's Report. John Ainsworth, Report by the P.C. Kisumu to H.E. the Governor on the Recent Kisii Revolt and Its Suppression, 1908, C.O. 533/42, London: Public Record Office.

Akama, J. S., 2017. *The Gusii of Kenya: Social, Economic, Cultural, Political & Judicial Perspectives.* Nsemia Inc. Publishers.

Executive Council. Minutes of the Executive Council, 15 January 1908. C.O. 544/1. London: Public Record Office.

Foran, W.R., 1936. *A Cuckoo in Kenya.* London: Hutchinson.

Jenkins, 1905. E. V. Jenkins, General Report on the Kisii Patrol, December 1905, C. O. 534/1, London: Public Relations Office.

Intelligence Report, 1905. Intelligence Report, 3rd Kings African Rifles for 19 September, 1905, C.O. 543/1, London: Public Record Office.

History of the WaKisii or Abagusii, 24 May 1916, DC/KSI/3/2. Nairobi: Kenya National Archives.

History of Kisii, 1907. History of Kisii District. DC/KSI/3/4. Nairobi: Kenya National Archives.

Hobley, C. W. 1902. *Eastern Uganda: An Ethnological Survey.* London: Anthropological Institute of Great Britain and Ireland.

Lonsdale, J. M. 1977. *The Politics of Conquest: The British in Western Kenya, 1894-1908*, The Historical Journal, XX: 841-70.

Mackay's Report. Report on Operations Against the Rebellious Sections of the Kisii tribe, 1 April 1908, C.O. 533/43, London: Public Record Office.

Manning 1905. Minute by Manning, 30 September 1905, on Stewart to Lyttleton, 8 June 1905, C.O. 533/2.

Matson, A. T. 1958. "Uganda's old Eastern Province and East Africa's Federal Capital", *Uganda Journal* 20: 43-53.

Maxon, Robert M. 1989, *Conflict and Accommodation in Western Kenya, the Gusii and the British, 1905-1963*. London: Associated Universities Press.

Mungeam, G. H. 1966. *British Rule in Kenya, 1985-1912*. London: Oxford University Press.

Munro, J. F. 1975. *Colonial Rule and the Kamba*. London: Oxford University Press.

Northcote's Diary. Diary of G.A.S. Northcote, 1907-08. DC/KSI/4/1. Nairobi: Kenya National Archives.

Nyanza Report, 1905-06. Report of the Province of Kisumu for the Year 1905-06, PC/NZA/1/4. Nairobi: Kenya National Archives.

Nyanza Special Report. Nyanza Special Report, 31 December 1909. PC/NZA/1/4. Nairobi: Kenya National Archives

Ochieng' W., 1974. *A Pre-colonial History of the Gusii of Western Kenya*. 1500 to 1914. Nairobi: East Africa Literature Bureau.

Omwenga, P. 1969. Field Interview in Gusii Region by Robert Maxon, 25 May 1969.

Ongaro, Mzee. 1969. Field Interview in Gusii region by Robert Maxon, 25 May 1969.

Partington, H. B. 1905. "Some notes on the Kisii people", *East Africa Quarterly*, 2: 328-29.

Shoenbron, D. L. 1998, A Green Place, A Good Place: Agrarian Change, Gender and Social Identity in the Great Lake Region. Nairobi: East Africa Educational Publishers.

Woodward, E. M. 1902. *Precis of Information Concerning Uganda* Protectorate London: His Majesty's Stationery Office.

www.ingramcontent.com/pod-product-compliance
Lightning Source LLC
Chambersburg PA
CBHW031400160426
43196CB00007B/841